AIR FRYER
COOKBOOK

GOOD
HOUSEKEEPING

AIR FRYER
COOKBOOK

70 DELICIOUS RECIPES

★ GOOD FOOD GUARANTEED ★

HEARST
books

HEARSTBOOKS

An Imprint of Sterling Publishing Co., Inc.
1166 Avenue of the Americas
New York, NY 10036

ISBN 978-1-61837-285-7

The Good Housekeeping Cookbook Seal guarantees that the recipes in this publication meet the strict standards of the Good Housekeeping Institute. The Institute has been a source of reliable information and a consumer advocate since 1900, and established its seal of approval in 1909. Every recipe in this publication has been triple-tested for ease, reliability, and great taste by the Institute.

Hearst Communications, Inc. has made every effort to ensure that all information in this publication is accurate. However, due to differing conditions, tools, and individual skills, Hearst Communications, Inc. cannot be responsible for any injuries, losses and/or damages that may result from the use of any information in this publication.

Distributed in Canada by Sterling Publishing
c/o Canadian Manda Group, 664 Annette Street
Toronto, Ontario, M6S 2C8, Canada
Distributed in Australia by NewSouth Books
45 Beach Street, Coogee, NSW 2034, Australia

For information about custom editions, special sales, and premium and corporate purchases, please contact Sterling Special Sales at 800-805-5489 or specialsales@sterlingpublishing.com.

Manufactured in China

8 10 9

goodhousekeeping.com
sterlingpublishing.com

Cover design by David Ter-Avanesyan
Interior design by Sharon Jacobs and Yeon Kim
For photography credits, see page 126

contents

HERB-ROASTED ROOT
VEGETABLES (PAGE 97)

Foreword

In my kitchen, countertop appliances have to earn their space. Meet the latest candidate, the air fryer.

With buzz building from tweens, and busy moms and dads, we started testing new and upcoming models in the Good Housekeeping Kitchen Appliances and Technology Lab.

Initial tests showed that air fryers do an excellent job crisping frozen packaged foods like fries and fried chicken and fish and spring rolls. I don't eat a lot of fried food, so when testing began, I put the air fryer in the "don't need, don't want" category.

And then we started doing more tests. We did fries from scratch, fried chicken, and cod cakes. And then we roasted: wings, Brussels sprouts, acorn squash, tofu, and meatballs. And then we tried veggie chips, hot dips, corn on the cob, and doughnuts. Suddenly the buzz made sense. This is "the little appliance that could."

In this collection of 70 triple-tested recipes from the Good Housekeeping Test Kitchens, you'll find appetizers and snacks like Warm Cheddar Corn Dip (page 43), Zucchini Tots (page 16), Cauliflower Popcorn (page 20), Three-Ingredient Pretzel Bites (page 26), and Air-Fried Chicken Wings (page 36) with 5 unique sauces. For dinner, check out Crispy Cod Cakes with Almond-Pepper Vinaigrette (page 46), Speedy Eggplant Parm (page 59), "Fried" Avocado Tacos (page 60), Mozzarella-Stuffed Turkey Meatballs (page 81), Bacon-Wrapped Pork Tenderloin (page 90), and more. Sides dishes, both roasted and fried, are a cinch in the air fryer: Fried Green Tomatoes (page 104), Roasted Sweet & Sour Brussels Sprouts (page 101), Summer Veggie Roast (page 108), Sweet Potato Fries (page 107), Crispy Roasted Potatoes (page 98), Polenta Fries (page 111), and more. And yes there are even breakfast and dessert options like Shortcut Jelly Doughnuts (page 114), Sweet 'n' Salty Maple Granola Bark (page 120), Fresh Fruit Crumble (page 117), Individual Apple Pies (page 118), and Individual Chocolate Molten Cakes (page 122).

I know that trying a new appliance can be a bit daunting, so our introduction provides easy to use instructions that will ensure great results. Plus, you'll find tips scattered throughout the book that add insider info for the air fryer and beyond.

Whenever I use the air fryer, I'm wowed that I'm cutting fat, adding flavor, and getting yummy results. Let the *Air Fryer Cookbook* be your guide to making healthier, delicious, convenient meals and snacks. Maybe it will even earn a permanent place on your counter. Ready, set, cook—and enjoy.

SUSAN WESTMORELAND
Food Director, *Good Housekeeping*

SPICY ACORN SQUASH WITH FETA (PAGE 96)

Introduction

What if we told you there was a machine that could fry foods into light and crispy perfection with little to no oil? Meet the air fryer. This cult-worthy countertop appliance cooks by circulating hot air around fries, chicken wings, and other fried favorites at a high speed, turning out crisp results with significantly less fat than what's used when cooking with a deep fryer. Technically, air fryers are mini convection ovens, though they work in a fraction of the time it would take your conventional oven and without heating up the whole house (read: a serious summertime game changer). With the turn of a dial, this trendy tool can fry up everything from bite-sized appetizers to weeknight main dishes in minutes—with all the flavor and none of the guilt.

MAXIMIZE YOUR MODEL

Most models have a drawer that pulls out, with a metal basket inside. Just toss your food in a bowl with a couple of tablespoons of oil, place the oil-coated food in the basket, and then set the temperature dial and the timer to cook. But before you start air-frying, be sure to follow these simple steps for the best results:

1. Don't overcrowd the fryer basket. In fact, the results are best when you arrange foods in a single layer, if possible. This ensures a light and crispy, non-soggy exterior.

2. Begin to air-fry your food within a few minutes of tossing in the oil.

3. Gently shake smaller ingredients in the fryer basket halfway through cooking (or every five to ten minutes) to help prevent them from frying unevenly and enhance their crispy texture.

4. When converting a recipe for something roasted or baked into an air fryer–friendly recipe, lower the temperature by 25°F but keep the cooking time the same.

5. Pre-packaged frozen foods don't need additional oil before being air-fried.

6. Most air fryer models have a basket with a nonstick coating, so avoid scraping the surface with metal utensils to preserve the finish.

7. Use caution when preparing highly greasy foods (like sausages) in the air fryer, as excessive fat dripping into the pan can cause smoking.

8. It's okay to pull the basket out at any time throughout the cooking cycle to check on the progress—most models will automatically shut off while the basket is out and resume when it's pushed back in. If food isn't sufficiently fried when the timer goes off, set the timer for a few extra minutes and continue cooking.

9. Always set the basket, pan, and any accessories on a heat-resistant surface when frying is complete. Use caution, as these tools get very hot during the cooking process.

10. When air-frying larger or delicate foods use tongs to lift them out of the fryer basket. Otherwise, you can turn the food out directly onto a serving bowl or platter.

11. Once food is removed, the air fryer is ready for another batch. But if you've been prepping fatty ingredients and excess oil has collected in the bottom of the basket, carefully pour it out after each batch.

12. You can also use your air fryer to reheat foods. Place food in the basket and set the temperature to 300°F for up to ten minutes.

13. Use a refillable oil mister spray can for coating foods, rather than nonstick cooking spray. Propellants in nonstick sprays can cause a residue to stick to cooking surfaces.

GOOD HOUSEKEEPING LAB PICKS

The Kitchen Appliance and Technology Lab at the Good Housekeeping Institute rigorously tested six air fryers for their ability to cook both homemade and frozen French fries, chicken nuggets, and breaded eggplant. We looked at taste and texture, noting crispness, tenderness, moisture, and evenness of browning. We also performed usability evaluations to assess the helpfulness of the manual and ease of using and reading the fryers' controls, presence or absence of variable temperature settings and an audible alert for when cooking is complete, how easy the fryer basket was to insert and remove, and cleanability. These are the lab's top-tested models.

TOP TESTED

BLACK + DECKER'S PURIFRY air fryer touts dual convection fans, knobs for setting cook time and temperature, and two indicator lights to show when the device is on and when it's preheated. It was exceptional at making crispy, well-browned frozen fries and chicken nuggets that were super tender on the inside. This model earned near-perfect ratings in ease of use evaluations, too, and all removable parts are dishwasher safe. It's available in black or white.

FEATURE-PACKED FRYER

THE PHILIPS AVANCE COLLECTION air fryer is decked out with bells and whistles, like preset programs for making frozen fries, meat, fish, and drumsticks, an LED-lit digital display, and a keep-warm function that works for up to thirty minutes. It also comes with a splatter-proof lid and a recipe booklet, and it works with a compatible Philips Airfryer app that has over two hundred recipes. Eggplant, fries, and chicken nuggets came out nicely browned and crisp in our testing.

SWEET & SPICY NUTS
(PAGE 40)

CLEANING YOUR AIR FRYER

Follow these easy instructions to keep your air fryer looking and smelling like new. But first, be sure that the appliance is off, unplugged, and cool.

CLEANING THE FRYER BASKET AND PAN:

1. Fill the pan with hot water and add a few drops of dishwashing soap. Allow the pan, with the basket inside, to soak for ten minutes.

2. After ten minutes, wipe the basket walls and bottom, plus the pan, with a moist cloth or a nonabrasive sponge.

3. Allow both the basket and the pan to air-dry before putting them back into the device. Many models have dishwasher-safe parts.

WASHING THE EXTERIOR: Clean the outside of the air fryer with a moist cloth, as well as the walls of the interior cavity that hold the fryer basket. If necessary, food residues stuck to the heating element inside may be removed with a nonabrasive sponge or a soft-bristle brush and wiped dry with a paper towel. Avoid steel wool or hard-bristle brushes, as these tools can damage the coating on the heating element.

OUR TEN FAVORITE FOODS TO AIR-FRY.

When testing recipes for this book, these were the dishes we could not get enough of!

1. **SHORTCUT JELLY DOUGHNUTS** (PAGE 114)

2. **AIR-FRIED CHICKEN WINGS** (PAGE 36)

3. **POLENTA FRIES** (PAGE 111)

4. **CHICKEN CAPRESE** (PAGE 73)

5. **MOZZARELLA EN CARROZZA** (PAGE 34)

6. **ROASTED SWEET & SOUR BRUSSELS SPROUTS** (PAGE 101)

7. **SWEET POTATO FRIES** (PAGE 107)

8. **CRISPY POTATOES WITH CAPER VINAIGRETTE** (PAGE 98)

9. **SHRIMP CURRY POTSTICKERS** (PAGE 19)

10. **CHIMICHURRI CAULIFLOWER "STEAKS"** (PAGE 103)

Air Fryer Cooking Guide

FOOD	TEMPERATURE	TIME	TIP
Baked Potato	400°F	25 minutes or until tender	Pierce skin of potato before cooking
Bread/Rolls	350°F	15–25 minutes	
Cake	325°F	15–25 minutes	
Chicken Breasts	350°F	10–15 minutes	
Chicken Drumsticks	350°F	20–25 minutes	
Chicken Nuggets	400°F	8–12 minutes	Shake halfway through
Fish	400°F	10–15 minutes	
Frozen Fries	400°F	12–20 minutes	Shake halfway through
Frozen Snacks (Spring Rolls, Chicken Wings, Fish Fillets, Onion Rings, etc.)	400°F	8–14 minutes or until hot	Shake halfway through
Hamburger	400°F	8–12 minutes	
Homemade Fries	400°F	15–24 minutes	Shake halfway through
Meatballs	350°F	10–15 minutes	
Mixed Veggies	350°F	8–12 minutes	Shake halfway through
Muffins	350°F	8–12 minutes	
Pork Chops	400°F	8–14 minutes	
Potato Wedges	350°F	18–25 minutes	Shake halfway through
Quiche	325°F	15–22 minutes	
Shellfish	350°F	7–15 minutes	

CREAMY BEER CHEESE WITH
AIR-FRIED SOFT PRETZELS
(PAGE 28)

1 | Apps & Snacks

With the air fryer, you can crisp up everything from frozen French fries to chicken wings to pizza rolls using just a tablespoon or two of oil. Now, you can enjoy your restaurant favorites, like jalapeño poppers, guilt-free! Get even healthier by subbing in good-for-you legumes and vegetables into your favorite recipes. Crunchy chickpea "nuts" are every bit as addictive as the traditional bar snack. When coated with Parmesan and turmeric or chili powder and lime zest and air-fried, cauliflower florets can easily stand in for popcorn next movie night. Plus, we will show you how you can use this countertop appliance to whip up classics, like baked ricotta, Stromboli, and pretzel bites.

Zucchini Tots

These spud-less tots are crispy on the outside, cheesy on the inside, and about to become your favorite way to use up surplus summer squash.

PREP: 15 MINUTES   TOTAL: 30 MINUTES

2 medium zucchini (about 12 ounces)

1 large egg

½ cup grated pecorino romano cheese

½ cup panko (Japanese-style bread crumbs)

1 clove garlic, crushed with press

¼ teaspoon black pepper

1. Shred zucchini and squeeze dry with paper towels. Mix the zucchini with egg, pecorino, panko, garlic, and pepper.

2. Use a small cookie scoop to drop tablespoonfuls onto a cutting board, and shape into 1-inch logs.

3. Preheat air fryer to 375°F. Spray basket with oil. Working in batches, place half the tots in the basket and air-fry until golden brown, 6 minutes.

SERVES 8 (3 tots each): About 70 calories, 5g protein, 5g carbohydrates, 3g fat (2g saturated), 1g fiber, 150mg sodium.

> **TIP**
>
> Air-frying is convection cooking on steroids, circulating hot air in a concentrated space. The perforated basket allows air to surround the food, cooking much faster on all surfaces. This concentrated air movement provides quick, even browning as well.

Shrimp Curry Potstickers

Don't be intimidated! Thanks to store-bought wrappers, it's easier than ever to make restaurant-quality dumplings at home. Feel free to use this method and experiment with different fillings.

PREP: 30 MINUTES   TOTAL: 50 MINUTES

½ **pound peeled and deveined shrimp, finely chopped**

1 medium zucchini, coarsely grated (about ½ cup)

1 tablespoon green curry paste

1 tablespoon fish sauce

¼ **cup basil, chopped**

2 scallions, thinly sliced

Round dumpling wrappers (about 30)

½ **tablespoon canola oil**

Oil in mister

1. Prepare filling: Stir together shrimp, zucchini, curry paste, fish sauce, basil, and scallions.

2. Place 1 rounded teaspoon of the filling in the center of 1 wrapper. Using your fingers, lightly wet edges of wrapper with water. Fold in half and press to seal, pleating as desired. Transfer sealed dumpling to greased and floured or parchment-lined baking sheet. Repeat with remaining filling and wrappers.

3. Preheat air fryer to 350°F. Combine ½ tablespoon oil and ¼ cup water in a small dish. Spray basket with oil. Working in batches, place one-third of potstickers in basket and brush with oil-and-water mixture. Air-fry until golden brown and crisp, 5 minutes.

4. Serve with Thai Lime Dipping Sauce (recipe below).

SERVES 10 (3 potstickers each): About 80 calories, 6g protein, 11g carbohydrates, 1g fat (0g saturated), 1g fiber, 455mg sodium.

Thai Lime Dipping Sauce

In a small bowl, stir together **1 tablespoon water, 1 tablespoon lime juice, 2 teaspoons fish sauce, 1 teaspoon low-sodium soy sauce**, and **1 teaspoon green curry paste**. Serve with potstickers.

Cauliflower "Popcorn"

This movie muncher has blockbuster health benefits—loads of immune-boosting vitamin C, potassium, cancer-fighting phytonutrients, and 2 grams of fiber per cup.

PREP: 15 MINUTES   TOTAL: 30 MINUTES

8 cups small cauliflower florets (about 1¼ pounds)

3 tablespoons olive oil

1 teaspoon garlic powder

½ teaspoon turmeric

½ teaspoon salt

¼ cup grated Parmesan cheese

1. Preheat air fryer to 390°F.

2. Toss cauliflower florets with olive oil, garlic powder, turmeric, and salt. Place in basket and air-fry until browned and tender, 15 minutes, shaking basket twice.

3. Toss with grated Parmesan cheese and serve immediately.

SERVES 8 (5 cups yield): About 85 calories, 3g protein, 6g carbohydrates, 6g fat (1g saturated), 2g fiber, 198mg sodium.

FUN FLAVORS

Truffle

Omit Parmesan, garlic powder, and turmeric. Toss roasted cauliflower with **2 tablespoons truffle butter** and **½ teaspoon pepper** before serving.

Chili Lime

Substitute **1 teaspoon chili powder** for Parmesan and turmeric. Grate **zest of 1 lime** over roasted cauliflower before serving.

TIP

Want to make a smaller serving? Cut the recipe in half and air-fry for 9 minutes.

Prosciutto-Wrapped Asparagus

The air fryer helps tackle the trickiest part of preparing these spring appetizers—getting the prosciutto crispy, without overcooking the asparagus.

PREP: 25 MINUTES   TOTAL: 35 MINUTES

12 slices thin prosciutto

½ cup freshly grated Parmesan cheese

24 asparagus spears, trimmed to fit the fryer basket

¼ teaspoon coarsely ground black pepper

1. Working in batches, place prosciutto on cutting board; cut each slice lengthwise in half and separate slightly. Sprinkle 1 teaspoon Parmesan on each prosciutto strip. Place 1 asparagus spear, angled, at end of 1 strip. Wrap prosciutto in spiral along length of asparagus (don't cover asparagus tip). Repeat with remaining prosciutto, Parmesan, and asparagus. Sprinkle with pepper. If not serving right away, cover and refrigerate up to 6 hours.

2. Preheat air fryer to 390°F. Place asparagus in crisscrossed layers (leaving space between the spears) in the basket. Air-fry until asparagus spears are just tender and prosciutto is crisped, 6 to 8 minutes.

3. Arrange on a platter and serve warm.

SERVES 12 (2 spears each): About 50 calories, 6g protein, 2g carbohydrates, 3g fat (1g saturated), 0g fiber, 391mg sodium.

Spiced Apple Wedges with Yogurt

Dehydrating apple slices takes hours. Thanks to the air fryer, you can enjoy this healthy snack in minutes.

PREP: **10 MINUTES**   TOTAL: **20 MINUTES**

2 medium apples, cored and sliced into ¼-inch wedges

1 teaspoon canola oil

2 teaspoons peeled and grated fresh ginger

½ teaspoon ground cinnamon

½ cup low-fat Greek vanilla yogurt, for serving

1. Preheat air fryer to 360°F. Toss apples with oil, ginger, and cinnamon. Place in basket and air-fry until tender, 12 minutes.

2. Serve with yogurt.

SERVES 4 (½ cup each): About 90 calories, 2g protein, 17g carbohydrates, 2g fat (0g saturated), 2g fiber, 15mg sodium.

TIP

Make an extra batch of Spiced Apple Wedges to keep in the fridge for future snacking.

Chickpea "Nuts"

Those chickpeas hiding in your pantry are about to become your new favorite munchie. Sprinkle them over salads, add to soups, or eat them by the handful.

PREP: 10 MINUTES   TOTAL: 25 MINUTES

2 (15-ounce) cans chickpeas
1 tablespoon olive oil
¼ teaspoon salt
¼ teaspoon pepper

1. Rinse and drain chickpeas; place on paper towels to absorb any excess water. Toss chickpeas, oil, salt, and pepper until evenly coated.

2. Preheat air fryer to 400°F. Place chickpeas in basket and air-fry until crisp, 23 minutes, shaking basket twice. Remove from fryer and transfer to a bowl; toss with seasonings (variations below), if desired. Chickpeas will continue to crisp as they cool. Cool completely and store in an airtight container.

SERVES 8 (¼ cup each): About 105 calories, 5g protein, 15g carbohydrates, 3g fat (0g saturated), 4g fiber, 201mg sodium.

FUN FLAVORS

Honey-Sesame

Toss **roasted chickpeas** in **2 tablespoons honey; 1 tablespoon each sesame oil, sesame seeds,** and **sugar;** and ½ **teaspoon each garlic powder** and **five-spice powder**. Place a square of foil coated with oil spray in basket and add coated chickpeas. Air-fry until caramelized and crisp, 6 to 8 minutes, shaking basket twice.

BBQ

Toss **roasted chickpeas** in **1 teaspoon dark brown sugar** and ½ **teaspoon each ground cumin, smoked paprika, garlic powder,** and **chili powder**.

Masala

Toss **roasted chickpeas** in ½ **teaspoon each garam masala, ground cumin,** and **ground ginger,** and ¼ **teaspoon cayenne (ground red) pepper**. Return to air fryer for 4 minutes until dry and crisp.

Spicy Buffalo

Toss **roasted chickpeas** in ¼ **cup cayenne pepper hot sauce**. Return to air fryer for 5 minutes until dry and crisp.

Maple-Cinnamon

Toss **roasted chickpeas** in **2 tablespoons maple syrup, 2 teaspoons sugar, 1 teaspoon ground cinnamon,** and ¼ **teaspoon ground nutmeg**. Return to air fryer for 5 minutes until caramelized and crisp.

Parmesan-Herb

Toss **roasted chickpeas** in ¼ **cup finely grated Parmesan** and **1 teaspoon each garlic powder, finely chopped fresh rosemary,** and **loosely packed lemon zest**.

Three-Ingredient Pretzel Bites

Craving something sweet? Skip the sea salt and coat dough balls with cinnamon sugar before placing them in the air fryer.

PREP: 15 MINUTES   TOTAL: 35 MINUTES

1 pound refrigerated pizza dough
⅓ cup baking soda
1 egg, beaten
Coarse salt, for sprinkling
Green onions and grainy mustard, for serving

1. Roll cherry-size pieces of pizza dough (about ½ ounce each) into balls. Boil 5 cups water in a medium-size pan. Take the pan off the stove and gradually stir in baking soda; bring to a simmer. Working in batches, add half the balls and cook 1 minute or until slightly puffed. With a slotted spoon, remove balls and place them on paper towels. Brush dough with egg; sprinkle with coarse salt.

2. Preheat air fryer to 350°F. Working in batches, place half the dough balls in the basket, spaced ½ inch apart. Air-fry until golden brown, about 10 minutes. Cool on a wire rack for at least 10 minutes.

3. Garnish with green onions and serve with grainy mustard.

SERVES 6 (5 bites each): About 185 calories, 5g protein, 32g carbohydrates, 3g fat (0g saturated), 1g fiber, 1,465mg sodium.

Creamy Beer Cheese with Air-Fried Soft Pretzels

Frozen pretzels taste soft, crisp, and delicious after being made in the air fryer. Serve this store-bought treat with our gooey, cheesy dip to make it feel more like a gourmet delicacy. See photo on page 14.

PREP: 10 MINUTES   TOTAL: 25 MINUTES

2 tablespoons butter

½ small onion, coarsely grated

¼ cup all-purpose flour

½ cup whole milk

1 (12-ounce) bottle pale ale

4 ounces cream cheese, at room temperature

1 tablespoon Dijon mustard

1 teaspoon Worcestershire sauce

½ teaspoon hot sauce (such as Tabasco)

1 pound sharp Cheddar cheese, coarsely grated

Air-Fried Frozen Soft Pretzels, for serving

1. Melt butter in a large saucepan on medium heat, then add onions and cook, stirring occasionally, until tender, 4 to 5 minutes. Sprinkle flour on top and cook, stirring, 1 minute.

2. Whisk in milk, then beer, and simmer, stirring occasionally, until mixture has thickened, 5 to 7 minutes. Stir in cream cheese, mustard, Worcestershire sauce, and hot sauce until melted and smooth.

3. Reduce heat to medium-low; add Cheddar in 3 additions, stirring each addition until melted before adding the next.

4. Serve warm with pretzels, if desired. Makes 4 cups.

SERVES 8 (½ cup each dip only): About 345 calories, 16g protein, 8g carbohydrates, 28g fat (15g saturated), 470mg sodium.

Air-Fried Frozen Soft Pretzels

Preheat air fryer to 350°F. Follow package directions for salting pretzels. Air-fry **frozen pretzels**, 2 or 3 at a time, for 3 to 4 minutes, or until hot.

Jalapeño Poppers

There's a reason you see these spicy stuffed peppers on almost every bar menu. Now you can easily add them to your air-frying repertoire.

PREP: 15 MINUTES   TOTAL: 40 MINUTES

2 slices bacon, halved

¾ cup whole milk ricotta cheese

½ cup shredded sharp Cheddar cheese

1 green onion, finely chopped

¼ teaspoon salt

6 large jalapeños, halved lengthwise and seeded

½ cup finely crushed potato chips

1. Preheat air fryer to 400°F. Lay bacon in single layer in basket. Air-fry bacon 5 minutes, or until crisp. Remove bacon and place on paper towels to drain. When cool, finely chop.

2. Stir together ricotta, Cheddar, green onion, bacon, and salt. Spoon into jalapeños; top with potato chips.

3. Place half the jalapeños in the basket and air-fry 8 minutes, or until tender. Repeat with the remaining jalapeños.

SERVES 6: About 150 calories, 7g protein, 6g carbohydrates, 11g fat (5g saturated), 1g fiber, 247mg sodium.

Roasted Onion Dip and Naan Chips

Roast, sauté, or grill onions before mixing them into creamy dips and salads, and they'll have a more subdued, sweeter flavor.

PREP: 20 MINUTES   TOTAL: 45 MINUTES, PLUS CHILLING

1 medium sweet onion, cut into ½-inch-thick slices

1 tablespoon olive oil

1 teaspoon fresh thyme leaves, chopped

¼ teaspoon pepper

2 large cloves garlic, unpeeled

4 ounces cream cheese, softened

½ cup low-fat sour cream

¼ cup mayonnaise

2 tablespoons lemon juice

1 tablespoon Worcestershire sauce

¾ teaspoon salt

3 large naan

Oil in mister

1. Separate onion slices into rings. In a bowl, toss onion rings with oil, thyme, and ¼ teaspoon pepper.

2. Preheat air fryer to 380°F. Place onions and garlic in basket and air-fry for 12 minutes, or until onion is tender and browned in spots, stirring a few times. Transfer onions and garlic to a cutting board; cool.

3. Prepare dip: Peel garlic and place in the bowl of a food processor; process until chopped. Add onions and pulse just until chopped. Add cream cheese, sour cream, mayonnaise, lemon juice, Worcestershire sauce, and salt; pulse until combined but not smooth. Transfer to a serving bowl. Refrigerate, covered, until cold. Makes about 1¾ cups.

4. Prepare Naan Chips: Cut naan into 2-inch squares; spray with oil. Preheat air fryer to 380°F. Air-fry the naan in 3 batches for 4 to 5 minutes, or until deep golden brown, turning a few times with tongs. Cool completely. Store in airtight container up to 1 week.

5. Serve dip with Naan Chips.

SERVES 7: About 275 calories, 5g protein, 26g carbohydrates, 16g fat (5g saturated), 1g fiber, 464mg sodium.

Stromboli

For a guest-worthy presentation, slice the sandwich, artfully arrange the slices on a platter, and serve with warmed marinara sauce.

PREP: 25 MINUTES   TOTAL: 45 MINUTES

4 large cloves garlic, unpeeled

½ cup marinated, pitted green and black olives

½ cup packed fresh basil leaves

3 tablespoons grated Parmesan cheese

¼ teaspoon crushed red pepper

½ pound pizza dough, at room temperature

¼ pound sliced provolone cheese (about 8 slices)

Olive oil in mister

1. Preheat air fryer to 370°F. Place garlic in basket; air-fry for 8 to 10 minutes, or until soft. Let cool.

2. Peel garlic and place in food processor; pulse until finely chopped. Add olives, basil, 2 tablespoons Parmesan, and red pepper. Pulse until finely chopped.

3. On a lightly floured surface, with a floured rolling pin, roll dough to a 14 x 8-inch rectangle. Cut rectangle in half crosswise. Working with one piece at a time, sprinkle ½ olive mixture over dough, up to ½-inch from edges. Arrange half of provolone over olive mixture, overlapping the cheese slices as necessary. Brush one long side with water. Roll up from opposite long side. Press seam to seal. Turn roll seam side down; pinch ends and tuck under. Make 3 shallow diagonal slashes on top. Repeat with the remaining dough, olive mixture, and provolone. Spray rolls with olive oil in a mister, and sprinkle with remaining Parmesan cheese.

4. Preheat air fryer to 370°F. Spray basket with olive oil in a mister. Place rolls in basket. Air-fry for 15 minutes, or until well browned. With spatula, remove rolls and place them on a rack to cool for 10 minutes.

5. Cut into four slices each with a serrated knife. Serve warm.

SERVES 8: About 150 calories, 6g protein, 14g carbohydrates, 7g fat (3g saturated), 1g fiber, 565mg sodium.

FUN FLAVOR
—
Ham & Cheese Stromboli

Follow directions for rolling and cutting dough. Top dough with ¼ **pound deli-sliced ham**, and **1 cup shredded Jarlsberg cheese**, mixed with **2 tablespoons Parmesan cheese** and **1 teaspoon chopped rosemary**, and **2 ounces deli-sliced hard salami**, dividing mixture evenly between dough halves, ½ inch from edges. Follow directions for shaping. Spray with **olive oil** and sprinkle with **1 tablespoon Parmesan cheese**. Follow directions for baking and cooling.

Baked Ricotta

Stash the leftovers in the fridge to use as a sandwich spread
for the rest of the week.

PREP: **10 MINUTES**   TOTAL: **25 MINUTES**

1 (15-ounce) container whole milk
    ricotta cheese

3 tablespoons grated Parmesan cheese

2 tablespoons extra-virgin olive oil

1 teaspoon fresh thyme leaves, chopped

1 teaspoon grated lemon zest

1 clove garlic, crushed with press

¼ teaspoon salt

¼ teaspoon pepper

Toasted Baguette Slices or crackers,
    for serving

TIP

Easily get baking dishes in and out of the
air fryer by making an aluminum foil "sling":
Fold a 24-inch piece of foil lengthwise into
thirds. Then, place under the dish and use
the sling to lift the dish into the air fryer.

1. Preheat air fryer to 380°F. To get the baking
dish in and out of the air fryer, create a sling
using a 24-inch length of foil, folded lengthwise
into thirds.

2. Whisk together ricotta, 2 tablespoons
Parmesan, oil, thyme, lemon zest, garlic, salt,
and pepper. Pour into a 6-inch, 3-cup ovenproof
baking dish; cover dish tightly with foil.

3. Place sling under dish and lift by the ends into
the air fryer, tucking the ends of the sling around
the dish. Air-fry for 10 minutes. Remove foil
cover and sprinkle with remaining 1 tablespoon
Parmesan. Air-fry for 5 more minutes, or until
bubbly at edges and top is browned.

4. Serve warm with toasted baguette slices
or crackers.

MAKES 2 CUPS (each ¼ cup): About 135 calories,
7g protein, 2g carbohydrates, 11g fat (5g saturated),
0g fiber, 139mg sodium.

Toasted Baguette Slices

Preheat air fryer to 350°F. Toast **twelve ¼-inch-
thick baguette slices** at a time. Spray 1 side of
slices with **olive oil**. Air-fry for 4 to 5 minutes,
tossing a few times with tongs, until lightly
toasted. Repeat in batches, if needed.

Mozzarella en Carrozza

Think of this melty sandwich as grilled cheese's flavor-packed Italian cousin.

PREP: 25 MINUTES   TOTAL: 30 MINUTES

1 plum tomato, seeded and chopped

2 tablespoons extra-virgin olive oil

1 tablespoon chopped fresh basil leaves

1 tablespoon capers, drained and chopped

1 teaspoon fresh lemon juice

⅜ teaspoon salt

4 ounces fresh mozzarella cheese, sliced

4 slices firm white bread, crusts trimmed

1 egg

2 tablespoons all-purpose flour

½ cup panko bread crumbs

3 tablespoons grated Parmesan cheese

Olive oil in mister

1. Mix together tomato, oil, basil, capers, lemon juice, and ⅛ teaspoon salt to make tomato vinaigrette. Set aside.

2. Place mozzarella between bread slices, making 2 sandwiches. Cut each sandwich in half diagonally.

3. Beat egg in a shallow dish. Mix together flour and ¼ teaspoon salt in another dish. Mix together panko and Parmesan in another dish. Dip sandwich halves, one at a time, into flour mixture to coat on all sides. Shake off excess flour. Dip in egg, and then in panko mixture, pressing panko to stick.

4. Preheat air fryer to 390°F. Spray air fryer basket with olive oil. Spray sandwiches on all sides with olive oil. Arrange in basket. Air-fry for 5 minutes, or until crisp and browned, turning once with tongs.

5. Cut each in half, making 8 triangles. Serve while hot with tomato vinaigrette.

SERVES 4: About 295 calories, 11g protein, 23g carbohydrates, 18g fat (7g saturated), 1g fiber, 468mg sodium.

TIP

The sandwiches can also be made with deli-sliced mozzarella cheese, using 2 ounces per sandwich (about 3 slices). Don't trim the crusts first, however. Trim after assembling, in case the cheese needs to be trimmed, too. Fresh mozzarella leaked slightly; the deli-sliced mozzarella did not.

Meatball Pizza Rolls

With just four ingredients and less than an hour, you can have these crowd-pleasers ready for company.

PREP: 30 MINUTES   TOTAL: 50 MINUTES

½ **pound pizza dough, at room temperature**

1½ **cups shredded Italian cheese blend**

16 **fully cooked frozen meatballs, thawed**

1 **cup pizza sauce, heated**

> **TIP**
>
> If pizza dough resists rolling, let it sit for a few minutes before trying to roll it again. Use meat-balls that measure 1 to 1¼ inches in diameter.

1. Divide dough in half. On a lightly floured surface, with a floured rolling pin, roll one piece of dough to a 14 x 4-inch strip. Sprinkle ½ cup cheese over the dough, up to 1 inch from 1 long edge. Place 8 meatballs evenly down the long side of the cheese-topped dough, with about ½ inch in between. Brush the uncovered part of the dough with water. Cut the dough crosswise between the meatballs into strips. Starting at the meatball side, roll up dough and press seam to seal. Pinch 1 side of dough to seal. Repeat with the remaining dough half, meatballs, and ½ cup cheese.

2. Preheat air fryer to 370°F. Spray basket with oil. Arrange 8 rolls, sealed side down, in basket with space in between. Air-fry for 8 minutes, or until browned. Sprinkle with ¼ cup cheese. Air-fry for 1 minute more, or until cheese melts. Remove with spatula. Repeat with remaining roll and cheese.

3. Serve while warm with pizza sauce.

SERVES 8: About 455 calories, 21g protein, 23g carbohydrates, 31g fat (13g saturated), 1g fiber, 1,227mg sodium.

Air-Fried Chicken Wings

Score big with these guilt-free wings—no matter what sauce you choose.

PREP: 10 MINUTES   TOTAL: 50 MINUTES

2 pounds chicken wings, tips removed
⅛ teaspoon salt

1. Preheat air fryer to 400°F. Season the wings with salt.

2. Working in 2 batches, place half the chicken wings in the basket and air-fry until the skin is browned and cooked through (165°F), 15 minutes, turning the wings with tongs halfway through cooking. Combine both batches in the air fryer and cook for 4 minutes more. Transfer to a large bowl and toss with sauce until evenly coated.

3. Serve immediately.

SERVES 6 (4 pieces without sauces): About 180 calories, 17g protein, 0g carbohydrates, 12g fat (4g saturated), 0g fiber, 109mg sodium.

FUN FLAVORS

Bourbon Barbecue Sauce

In a 2-quart saucepan, combine ¾ **cup barbecue sauce,** ¼ **cup bourbon,** and **1 table-spoon yellow mustard.** Heat to simmering on medium-high heat; simmer 3 minutes, stirring. Transfer to a bowl; toss with cooked wings.

Sesame Teriyaki Sauce

In a large bowl, whisk together **3 tablespoons teriyaki sauce, 2 tablespoons rice vinegar, 1 tablespoon dark brown sugar,** and **2 teaspoons toasted sesame oil**; toss with cooked wings and **2 tablespoons sesame seeds.**

Buffalo Wings

In a 1-quart saucepan, melt **3 tablespoons butter** on medium heat. Whisk in ¼ **cup cayenne pepper sauce** and **2 tablespoons distilled white vinegar.** Toss with hot wings and serve with ¼ **cup blue cheese dip.**

Hot Caribbean Wings

In a 2-quart saucepan, mix **2 cups mango nectar, 2 teaspoons habañero hot sauce, 1 pinch allspice, ⅛ teaspoon salt,** and ⅛ **teaspoon black pepper.** Cook on medium-high heat for 8 minutes to reduce by half. Stir in **2 teaspoons lime juice.** Toss with hot cooked wings and garnish with ¼ **cup chopped cilantro.**

Sweet 'n' Sticky Thai Wings

In a medium-size bowl, place ½ **cup Thai sweet chili sauce, grated lime peel from 1 lime,** and **1 teaspoon fish sauce.** Stir well. Toss with hot cooked wings, and sprinkle on ⅓ **cup French-fried onions.**

BOURBON BARBECUE SAUCE

SWEET 'N' STICKY THAI WINGS

HOT CARIBBEAN WINGS

SESAME TERIYAKI SAUCE

BUFFALO WINGS

Bacon-Wrapped Barbecue Shrimp

When in doubt, wrap it with bacon.

24 large, peeled, and deveined shrimp,
    about ¾ pound

5 tablespoons barbecue sauce

12 strips bacon, cut in half

24 small pickled jalapeño slices

1. Toss together shrimp and 3 tablespoons barbecue sauce. Let stand 15 minutes. Soak 24 wooden toothpicks in water for 10 minutes. Wrap 1 piece bacon around shrimp and jalapeño slice, then secure with a toothpick.

2. Preheat air fryer to 350°F. Working in batches, place half of shrimp in the fryer basket, spacing them ½ inch apart. Air-fry for 10 minutes. Turn shrimp over with tongs and air-fry for 3 minutes more until bacon is golden brown and shrimp are cooked through.

3. Brush with the remaining barbecue sauce and serve.

SERVES 8 (3 pieces each): About 125 calories, 12g protein, 5g carbohydrates, 6g fat (2g saturated), 0g fiber, 661mg sodium.

TIP

Air fryer baskets are dishwasher-safe, providing splatter-free cooking with minimal cleanup.

Chili Nut Snack Mix

Keep a few essentials in your pantry, and you'll never be more than 30 minutes away from snack nirvana.

PREP: 10 MINUTES   **TOTAL:** 25 MINUTES

1 large egg white

2 tablespoons brown sugar

1 teaspoon chili powder

1 teaspoon salt

¾ teaspoon ground cayenne pepper

1 teaspoon smoked paprika, divided

1 cup unsalted natural almonds

1 cup pepitas

1½ cups bite-sized Cheddar crackers

1½ cups honey-wheat pretzel twists, cut into thirds

1. Whisk together egg white, brown sugar, chili powder, salt, cayenne, and ½ teaspoon smoked paprika in a large bowl until well blended. Toss in almonds, pepitas, crackers, and pretzel pieces until evenly coated.

2. Preheat air fryer to 350°F. Coat the basket with oil spray. Place the mix in the basket and air-fry until toasted, 10 to 12 minutes, stirring every 3 minutes for even browning. Place on a rimmed baking sheet, sprinkle with the remaining smoked paprika, and toss to combine. Spread out and cool completely.

3. Store in an airtight container for up to 2 weeks.

SERVES 8 (¼ cup each): About 375 calories, 13g protein, 39g carbohydrates, 21g fat (6g saturated), 5g fiber, 602mg sodium.

Sweet & Spicy Nuts

From sophisticated soirees to casual game-viewing parties (and everything in between!), mixed nuts are a menu *must*. See photo on page 11.

PREP: 10 MINUTES   TOTAL: 35 MINUTES

½ cup sugar

1 teaspoon salt

½ teaspoon ground cinnamon

½ teaspoon ground cumin

½ teaspoon black pepper

¼ teaspoon ground red pepper (cayenne)

1 large egg white

3 cups unsalted walnuts (or mixed nuts)

Oil in mister

1. In a small bowl, combine sugar, salt, cinnamon, cumin, black pepper, and red pepper; stir until blended. In a large bowl, with a wire whisk, beat egg white until foamy. Measure 1 tablespoon of the beaten egg white and set aside for another use or discard; keep the rest. Add nuts to egg white in the large bowl; stir to coat evenly. Add sugar mixture; toss until nuts are thoroughly coated.

2. Preheat air fryer to 300°F. Spray basket with oil and add nut mixture. Air-fry for 20 to 25 minutes, or until nuts are golden brown and dry, stirring nuts from bottom to top with a spatula a few times. Spread nuts out on baking sheet and let them cool completely.

3. Store in an airtight container at room temperature up to 1 month.

SERVES 8 (½ cup each): About 300 calories, 6g protein, 18g carbohydrates, 25g fat (2g saturated), 3g fiber, 247mg sodium.

Crispy Kale "Chips"

These are the epitome of a guilt-free snack.

8 cups deribbed kale leaves, torn into 2-inch pieces

1½ tablespoons olive oil

¾ teaspoon chili powder

½ teaspoon paprika

¼ teaspoon garlic powder

2 teaspoons sesame seeds

1. Preheat air fryer to 350°F. Toss together kale, oil, chili powder, paprika, garlic powder, and sesame seeds. Massage kale for 1 minute.

2. Place in the basket and air-fry until crisped, 8 minutes, turning kale twice with tongs.

3. Cool and store in an airtight container for up to 1 week.

SERVES 5 (1 cup each): About 60 calories, 1g protein, 3g carbohydrates, 5g fat (1g saturated), 1g fiber, 24mg sodium.

TIP

Don't cut the kale too small. As the kale dehydrates, smaller pieces can be easily blown around inside the air fryer.

Apple Chips

Nothing but fruit, these are a healthy alternative that will satisfy your craving for something sweet and crunchy.

PREP: 5 MINUTES   TOTAL: 40 MINUTES

1 honeycrisp or pink lady apple

1. Core apple with an apple corer, leaving apple whole. Cut apple into ⅛-inch-thick slices.

2. Preheat air fryer to 300°F. Arrange apple slices in the basket, staggering slices as much as possible. Air-fry for 25 to 35 minutes, or until chips are dry and some are lightly browned, turning 4 times with tongs to separate and rotate them from top to bottom. Place chips in a single layer on a wire rack to cool. Apples will become crisper as they cool.

SERVES 1: About 80 calories, 0g protein, 22g carbohydrates, 0g fat (0g saturated), 4g fiber, 0mg sodium.

TIP

Use the air fryer to supplement your favorite recipes, such as roasting peppers for pasta salad, toasting bread cubes to make croutons, or cooking bacon for quiche.

Warm Cheddar Corn Dip

Tortilla chips, meet your match! This melty cheese dip, made with homemade ranch dressing, will be the hit of the snack table.

PREP: 15 MINUTES   TOTAL: 55 MINUTES

4 ounces cream cheese, softened

¼ cup nonfat Greek yogurt

¼ cup low-fat milk

3 tablespoons mayonnaise

1 chipotle in adobo sauce, finely chopped (1 tablespoon)

¼ teaspoon garlic powder

1 cup frozen corn, thawed

1 cup shredded Mexican cheese blend, divided

2 tablespoons chopped fresh cilantro leaves

Air-Fried Tortilla Chips (recipe right), for serving

1. Beat cream cheese until smooth. Beat in yogurt, milk, mayonnaise, chipotle, and garlic powder until blended. Add corn and ¾ cup cheese; beat 1 minute on medium speed. Pour into a 6-inch-wide, 3-cup, ovenproof baking dish. Cover dish tightly with foil.

2. Preheat air fryer to 380°F. Make a sling out of foil. Place dish on the sling and put it in the basket. Air-fry for 30 minutes. Uncover and air-fry for 5 more minutes, or until dip is bubbly at the edges. Sprinkle with the remaining ¼ cup cheese and air-fry for 2 more minutes, or until cheese melts.

3. Top with cilantro and serve warm with tortilla chips.

SERVES 8 (¼ cup each): About 155 calories, 6g protein, 5g carbohydrates, 13g fat (6g saturated), 0g fiber, 147mg sodium.

Air-Fried Tortilla Chips

Preheat air fryer to 350°F. Spray **4 small corn tortillas** with **oil** and stack. Cut stack into pieces. Place in air fryer basket. Air-fry 6 minutes, or until deep golden brown, stirring twice. Let cool completely.

TIP

Cut tortillas into ¼-inch-wide strips before frying to make crispy croutons for salads and soups.

ULTIMATE FRIED CHICKEN
SANDWICH (PAGE 70)

2 | Main Dishes

While the air fryer works so well with the expected "fried" foods, it's much more versatile. Steaks, meatloaf, burgers, and meatballs especially benefit from this cooking method, as it allows them to brown up beautifully, while staying juicy and tender. Tofu gets deep-fried texture without any of the added oil, calories, or sogginess. Even chicken can be made in the air fryer! Check out our Mahogany Chicken & Broccoli recipe, if you need convincing. Craving something fried-and-true? We're also teaching you how to cook up crispy cod cakes, falafel, fried chicken, and fish 'n' chips—as well as what to serve each with to make it a delicious meal.

Crispy Cod Cakes with Almond-Pepper Vinaigrette

These cod poppers, topped with a savory vinaigrette, make for a satisfying meal when served over a bed of salad greens.

PREP: 15 MINUTES   TOTAL: 40 MINUTES

1 pound cod (or haddock) fillets, cut into chunks

⅓ cup packed fresh basil leaves

3 cloves garlic, crushed with press

½ teaspoon smoked paprika

¼ teaspoon salt

¼ teaspoon pepper

1 large egg, beaten

1 cup panko bread crumbs

Oil in mister

Almond-Pepper Vinaigrette (recipe at right)

Salad greens, for serving

1. In a food processor, pulse cod, basil, garlic, smoked paprika, salt, and pepper until cod is finely chopped, stirring occasionally. Form into 8 patties, about 2 inches in diameter. Dip each first into the egg, then into the panko, patting to adhere. Spray with oil on one side.

2. Preheat air fryer to 400°F. Working in batches, place half the cakes in the basket, oil side down; spray with oil. Air-fry for 12 minutes, until golden brown and cooked through.

3. Serve cod cakes with vinaigrette and salad greens.

SERVES 4: About 450 calories, 24g protein, 21g carbohydrates, 30g fat (4g saturated), 3g fiber, 470mg sodium.

Almond-Pepper Vinaigrette

In a blender, puree ⅓ **cup salted almonds, 5 tablespoons sherry vinegar, 5 tablespoons olive oil**, and ¼ **teaspoon salt** until smooth. Add ⅓ **cup roasted red peppers**; pulse until almost smooth.

Crab Cakes with Asian Slaw

A small amount of panko bread crumbs, plus the air fryer,
help make these hearty crab cakes extra crispy.

PREP: 20 MINUTES   TOTAL: 30 MINUTES

5 tablespoons light mayonnaise

1 teaspoon low-sodium soy sauce

8 ounces lump crabmeat

2 green onions, thinly sliced

1 large egg white

½ cup panko bread crumbs

Oil in mister

3 cups shredded red cabbage

2 tablespoons seasoned rice vinegar

1 teaspoon Asian sesame oil

½ teaspoon peeled and grated fresh ginger

1. In a small bowl, whisk 2 tablespoons mayonnaise with soy sauce; set soy mayonnaise aside for serving.

2. Pick over crabmeat to remove any pieces of shell or cartilage. In a medium-size bowl, mix half the green onions, egg white, 2 tablespoons panko, and remaining 3 tablespoons mayonnaise until blended. Stir in crabmeat. Shape into four 3-inch patties. Coat patties with remaining panko, pressing to adhere.

3. Preheat air fryer to 390°F to 400° F. Spray air fryer basket and both sides of crab cakes with oil. Air-fry for 10 minutes, or until crab cakes are golden and cooked through, turning once.

4. Meanwhile, in a large bowl, combine cabbage, vinegar, sesame oil, ginger, and remaining green onion to make a slaw. Serve crab cakes with Asian slaw and top with soy mayonnaise.

5. Serve any remaining mayonnaise on the side.

SERVES 2: About 390 calories, 26g protein, 34g carbohydrates, 17g fat (3g saturated), 3g fiber, 1,292mg sodium.

Crispy Potato Patties with Creole Shrimp

Mashed up too many potatoes? Turn those leftovers into tonight's dinner.

PREP: 20 MINUTES   TOTAL: 1 HOUR 5 MINUTES, PLUS FREEZING

3 cups cold leftover mashed potatoes

1 large egg, beaten

½ cup plain dried bread crumbs

2 large stalks celery

1 small green or red pepper

4 cloves garlic

Oil in mister

1 tablespoon vegetable oil

2 teaspoons salt-free Creole seasoning

1 (14.5-ounce) can diced tomatoes

1 pound shelled, deveined, large (20–24 count) shrimp

2 teaspoons Louisiana-style hot sauce

¼ teaspoon salt

Sliced green onions, for serving

1. Form potatoes into 8 (2½-inch-thick) patties. Brush tops with egg and sprinkle with half of crumbs, pressing to adhere. Turn patties over and repeat on the other side. Place patties on a large platter or cutting board and freeze for 20 minutes. Meanwhile, chop celery, pepper, and garlic.

2. Preheat air fryer to 390°F to 400°F. Spray basket with oil. Spray patties with oil. Air-fry patties, in 2 batches, for 10 minutes each batch, or until browned and crisp. Remove to platter.

3. Meanwhile, in a 4-quart saucepan, heat 1 tablespoon oil on medium heat. Add celery and pepper. Cook 5 minutes or until vegetables begin to soften, stirring occasionally. Add garlic and Creole seasoning. Cook 2 minutes, stirring. Add tomatoes. Heat to simmering. Reduce heat to maintain simmer. Simmer 10 minutes, stirring occasionally.

4. Add shrimp, hot sauce, and salt. Cook 5 minutes, or until shrimp are opaque throughout and cooked, stirring occasionally. Serve shrimp mixture over potato patties; garnish with green onions.

SERVES 4: About 430 calories, 27g protein, 46g carbohydrates, 14g fat (6g saturated), 5g fiber, 1,922mg sodium.

Crispy Fish Tacos

One bite and you'll *swear* you're in Southern California.

PREP: 20 MINUTES   **TOTAL:** 30 MINUTES

⅓ cup mayonnaise

2 tablespoons milk

1 teaspoon chili powder

¼ teaspoon garlic powder

1½ cups panko bread crumbs

4 teaspoons canola or vegetable oil

½ teaspoon salt

1 pound skinless mahi-mahi or tilapia fillets, cut into 3-inch-long strips (1 inch wide)

Oil in mister

Small (6-inch) flour tortillas

1. In a small bowl, whisk together mayonnaise, milk, chili powder, and garlic powder. On a plate, mix panko with oil and salt.

2. Working with a few strips at a time, toss fish in the mayonnaise mixture to coat and then toss them in panko, pressing to stick. Place coated strips on a baking sheet.

3. Preheat air fryer to 390°F to 400°F. Spray basket with oil. Arrange fish with space between strips, and stack strips perpendicular in a second layer. Air-fry fish in 2 batches, 4 to 5 minutes per batch, until cooked through.

4. Serve on flour tortillas with your choice of toppings (at right).

SERVES 4 (fish only): About 370 calories, 24g protein, 23g carbohydrates, 19g fat (3g saturated), 1g fiber, 525mg sodium.

FUN FLAVORS: TOPPINGS

Pineapple & Romaine Slaw

In a bowl, toss ¼ **small pineapple** (cut into ¼-inch pieces) and **2 thinly sliced green onions** with **1 tablespoon each lime juice** and **olive oil** and ¼ **teaspoon each salt and pepper**. Toss with ½ **heart romaine lettuce** (finely shredded; about 1½ cups) and ¼ **cup cilantro** (chopped).

Citrusy Radishes

In a bowl, whisk together **1 tablespoon each orange juice** and **lemon juice** and ¼ **teaspoon each ground cumin**, **salt**, and **pepper**. Add **6 radishes** (very thinly sliced), and ¼ **small sweet onion** (thinly sliced); toss to combine. Stir in ¼ **cup cilantro** before serving.

Cabbage Slaw

In a bowl, whisk together **2 tablespoons each sour cream** and **lime juice,** ⅛ **teaspoon cayenne,** and ¼ **teaspoon salt**. Toss with **2 cups shredded green or red cabbage**. Let stand, tossing often, for 10 minutes. Stir in **1 sliced green onion** and **2 tablespoons cilantro** (chopped).

TIP

It's OK to stack the fish while frying—just stack each layer perpendicular to the one below it.

Fish 'n' Chips

Channel the folks on the other side of the pond and cook up this crispy fish dish for dinner.

1½ pounds cod fillets, cut into strips

3 large egg whites, beaten

6 ounces salt-and-vinegar potato chips, finely crushed

½ teaspoon salt

1 pound frozen peas

3 tablespoons butter

1 tablespoon lemon juice

¼ teaspoon pepper

Lemon wedges and chives, for serving

1. Cut fish into equal-size pieces; fold thinner tail ends in half, if needed, and secure with a toothpick. Dip cod into egg white, then chips.

2. Preheat air fryer to 350°F. Working in batches, place half the fish in the basket and air-fry for 8 to 10 minutes until golden and cooked through. Sprinkle with ¼ teaspoon salt.

3. Meanwhile, microwave on High frozen peas, butter, lemon juice, and ¼ teaspoon each salt and pepper for 5 minutes. Puree in food processor.

4. Serve fish with pea puree, lemon wedges, and chives.

SERVES 4: About 320 calories, 39g protein, 40g carbohydrates, 25g fat (8g saturated), 7g fiber, 776mg sodium.

TIP

Crush chips right in the bag for less mess. Make a small hole in the top (so air can escape) and go to town with a rolling pin.

Garlic Shrimp Caesar Salad

Sub in Greek yogurt for the mayonnaise to lighten up this crowd-pleasing salad.

PREP: 15 MINUTES   **TOTAL:** 25 MINUTES

1 large lemon

1 pound shelled, deveined, large
(20–24 count) shrimp

1 tablespoon olive oil

3 garlic cloves, crushed with press

1 teaspoon hot paprika

⅜ teaspoon salt

Oil in mister

1 head romaine lettuce

1 head radicchio

¼ cup plain nonfat Greek yogurt

3 tablespoons finely grated Parmesan cheese

1 teaspoon Dijon mustard

¼ teaspoon pepper

1 cup prepared unseasoned croutons

1. From lemon, grate 1 teaspoon zest and squeeze 3 tablespoons juice. In a large bowl, toss shrimp, olive oil, 2 crushed garlic cloves, hot paprika, lemon zest, and ⅛ teaspoon salt.

2. Preheat air fryer to 390°F to 400°F. Spray basket with oil. Air-fry shrimp in 2 batches, in single layers, 3 minutes per batch, or until cooked (145°F).

3. Meanwhile, thinly slice romaine lettuce and radicchio, and place the greens in a large serving bowl. In a small bowl, whisk Greek yogurt, Parmesan cheese, mustard, 1 crushed garlic clove, lemon juice, and ¼ teaspoon each salt and pepper. Toss with lettuce mixture in bowl.

4. Top with shrimp and croutons.

SERVES 4: About 230 calories, 26g protein, 16g carbohydrates, 7g fat (2g saturated), 4g fiber, 1,170mg sodium.

Falafel with Cucumber-Tomato Salad

Pack up the pita, patties, and salad separately to bring this meal on-the-go.

PREP: 25 MINUTES   TOTAL: 45 MINUTES

1 lemon

¼ cup fresh mint leaves

3 cloves garlic

1 teaspoon ground cumin

1 teaspoon ground coriander

1 cup packed flat-leaf parsley

1⅛ teaspoons salt

½ teaspoon pepper

2 (15-ounce) cans chickpeas, rinsed and drained

3 tablespoons all-purpose flour

Oil in mister

⅓ cup tahini (sesame paste)

4 tablespoons extra-virgin olive oil

1 pound tomatoes, chopped

2 seedless (English) cucumbers, chopped

½ small red onion, finely chopped

Toasted pita bread, for serving

1. From lemon, grate 1 teaspoon peel and squeeze 3 tablespoons juice; set aside.

2. In a food processor bowl, place mint, garlic, cumin, coriander, lemon peel, ½ cup parsley, and ½ teaspoon each salt and pepper; pulse until finely chopped. Add chickpeas and flour; pulse until just chopped and well mixed, occasionally scraping down the side of the bowl with a rubber spatula.

3. With a measuring cup, scoop a scant ¼ cupful of mixture and shape into 12 (2-inch-diameter) patties. Spray tops of patties with oil.

4. Preheat air fryer to 400°F. Working in batches, place half of patties, oil side down, in basket; spray with oil. Air-fry 14 minutes, until golden brown.

5. Meanwhile, in a small bowl, whisk together tahini, 2 tablespoons olive oil, ½ cup cold water, and ⅛ teaspoon salt until smooth; set aside. In a large bowl, toss tomatoes with cucumbers, onion, reserved lemon juice, remaining ½ cup parsley, remaining 2 tablespoons olive oil, and ½ teaspoon salt.

6. Serve falafel with salad; drizzle with tahini sauce. Serve with toasted pita.

SERVES 6: About 340 calories, 11g protein, 33g carbohydrates, 19g fat (3g saturated), 9g fiber, 564mg sodium.

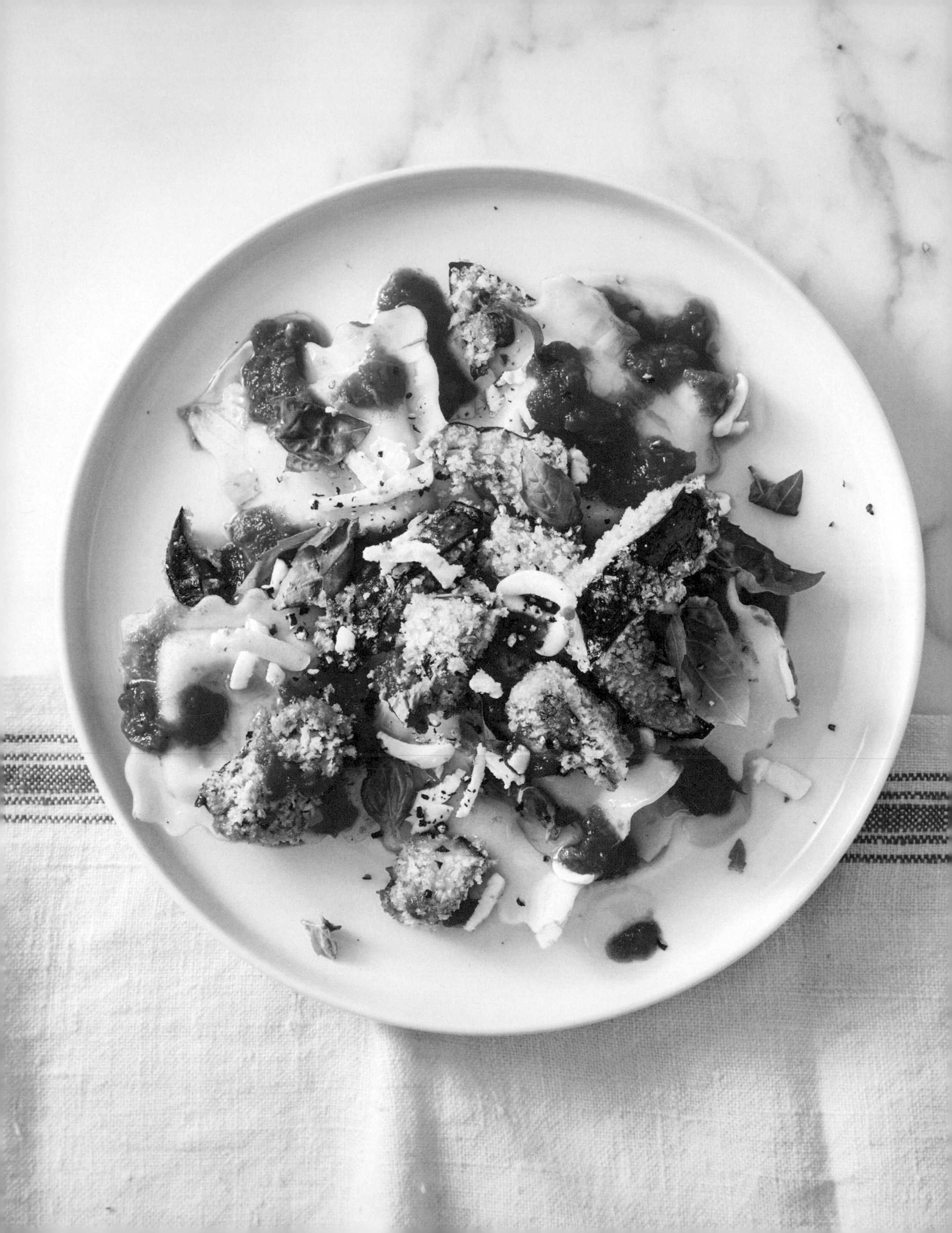

Speedy Eggplant Parm

Thanks to one special, shortcut ingredient (ravioli!), this Italian favorite is much more weeknight-friendly.

PREP: 20 MINUTES   **TOTAL:** 40 MINUTES

½ cup all-purpose flour

1 large egg

1 large egg white

¾ cup panko bread crumbs

½ cup freshly grated Parmesan cheese

½ teaspoon garlic powder

½ teaspoon kosher salt

¼ teaspoon pepper

1 small eggplant (about 12 ounces),
    cut into ½-inch-thick rounds

Oil in mister

1 (16- to 18-ounce) package cheese ravioli

1¼ cups marinara sauce, warmed

Shredded fresh mozzarella, for serving
    (optional)

1. Place flour on a plate. In a shallow bowl, beat 1 whole egg with 1 egg white. In a second shallow bowl, combine panko, Parmesan cheese, garlic powder, kosher salt, and pepper. Coat eggplant rounds in flour, then in egg (letting any excess drip off), then in panko mixture, pressing to adhere. Spray one side with oil.

2. Preheat air fryer to 400°F. Working in batches, place half of eggplant in basket, oil side down; spray with oil. (Slices may overlap slightly.) Air-fry until eggplant is tender and golden brown, 14 minutes. Once cooked, invert the first batch on top of the just-cooked slices in the basket. Air-fry for 2 minutes, just until heated. Turn off fryer and let the eggplant stand in the fryer until using.

3. Meanwhile, cook cheese ravioli as label directs. Drain, divide among serving plates, and top with marinara sauce. Cut eggplant into bite-sized pieces; scatter on top of ravioli. Top with shredded fresh mozzarella, if desired.

SERVES 4: About 500 calories, 22g protein, 65g carbohydrates, 16g fat (8g saturated), 6g fiber, 1,182mg sodium.

"Fried" Avocado Tacos

Take your avocado obsession to the next level by rolling avocado slices in bread crumbs, air-frying them to crispy perfection, and stuffing them in a tortilla.

PREP: 25 MINUTES   **TOTAL: 40 MINUTES**

¼ **cup all-purpose flour**

¼ **teaspoon salt, plus a pinch**

¼ **teaspoon pepper**

2 **large egg whites**

1¼ **cups panko bread crumbs**

2 **tablespoons olive oil**

2 **avocados, peeled and halved**

Oil in mister

1 **lime**

¼ **cup mayonnaise**

½ **small red cabbage, thinly sliced**

2 **green onions, thinly sliced**

1 **seeded jalapeño, thinly sliced**

½ **cup cilantro leaves**

Flour tortillas, warmed

Lime wedges and sour cream, for serving (optional)

1. In a small bowl, whisk flour with salt and pepper. Lightly beat egg whites in a second bowl. In a third bowl, combine panko with olive oil.

2. Cut avocados into ½-inch-thick slices. One at a time, coat slices in flour, then in egg, and then in panko, pressing gently.

3. Preheat air fryer to 390°F to 400° F. Spray basket with oil. Place avocado slices in the basket in a single layer. Air-fry in batches for 6 minutes, or until browned.

4. Meanwhile, finely grate zest from lime into a large bowl, then squeeze in 2 tablespoons lime juice. Whisk in mayonnaise and a pinch of salt. Add cabbage, green onions, and jalapeño; toss to coat. Fold in cilantro leaves.

5. Serve avocados and slaw in tortillas with lime wedges and sour cream, if desired.

SERVES 4: About 470 calories, 8g protein, 40g carbohydrates, 32g fat (5g saturated), 10g fiber, 335mg sodium.

TIP

Look for avocados that are firm-ripe, not the soft kind you'd buy to make guacamole.

Crispy Tofu Bowl

Vegetarians, rejoice! This meat-free staple tastes even better when cooked in an air fryer and served over a bed of greens, quinoa, rice, or ramen noodles.

PREP: 15 MINUTES   TOTAL: 45 MINUTES

14 ounces extra-firm tofu

½ small red onion, very thinly sliced

¼ cup red wine vinegar

¼ cup Thai sweet chili sauce

1 tablespoon olive oil

¼ teaspoon salt

1 seedless cucumber, chopped

½ cup cashew halves

3 tablespoons cornstarch

Oil in mister

1 cup quinoa, cooked

Parsley or cilantro leaves, for serving

TIP

Instead of the quinoa, you can serve tofu with cooked brown rice or ramen noodles.

1. Slice tofu ¼ inch thick. Place the tofu on a cutting board between paper towels; top with a baking sheet. Top with large cans or another weight; let stand 10 minutes. Soak red onion in cold water until ready to use.

2. Whisk red wine vinegar and Thai sweet chili sauce, olive oil, and salt. Pat onion dry; toss with half the vinaigrette and cucumber.

3. Preheat air fryer to 350°F. Air-fry cashews for 3 minutes, or until toasted; set aside. Sprinkle cornstarch on both sides of the tofu, rubbing the cornstarch with your fingers to coat the tofu. Spray both sides with oil.

4. Increase air fryer temperature to 390°F to 400°F. Spray basket with oil. Working in batches, place tofu in a single layer and air-fry for 10 to 12 minutes, turning once, until light golden brown and crisp.

5. Divide quinoa among 4 bowls. Top each with cucumber-onion salad, 2 tablespoons cashew halves, parsley or cilantro leaves, and tofu. Serve with remaining vinaigrette on the side.

SERVES 4: About 455 calories, 20g protein, 49g carbohydrates, 19g fat (3g saturated), 6g fiber, 280mg sodium.

Spinach & Cheese Breakfast Pockets

Double this recipe and freeze a few of these cheesy hand pies before baking. Whenever the craving hits, stick one into a 350°F air fryer for 15 to 18 minutes, or until golden brown.

PREP: 20 MINUTES   TOTAL: 1 HOUR 20 MINUTES

2 large eggs

1 cup ricotta cheese

1 cup baby spinach, roughly chopped

1 cup basil, chopped

¼ cup sun-dried tomatoes (about 9), finely chopped

¼ teaspoon red pepper flakes

¼ teaspoon kosher salt

2 refrigerated rolled piecrusts (from a 15-ounce box)

Sesame seeds, for sprinkling

1. Preheat air fryer to 375°F to 380°F. In a small bowl, whisk together 1 egg with 1 tablespoon water; set aside.

2. In a medium bowl, combine ricotta, spinach, basil, tomatoes, red pepper flakes, remaining egg, and kosher salt.

3. Unroll piecrusts and cut each into 4 wedges. Divide ricotta mixture among wedges (about 3 tablespoons for each), placing on 1 side, ½ inch from edges. Fold dough over filling and press edges with fork to seal.

4. Brush tops with egg mixture and sprinkle with sesame seeds. Air-fry in batches (2 at a time), 10 to 12 minutes, or until golden brown.

MAKES 8: About 285 calories, 8g protein, 27g carbohydrates, 8g fat (8g saturated), 1g fiber, 370mg sodium.

Veggie Wraps with Goat Cheese

Boost the flavor of portobellos, red peppers, and green beans by tossing them in the air fryer before adding them to the wrap.

2 portobello mushroom caps, sliced

1 large red pepper, sliced

8 ounces green beans

2 tablespoons olive oil

¼ teaspoon salt

1 (15-ounce) can chickpeas, drained

3 tablespoons lemon juice

¼ teaspoon pepper

4 (6-inch) whole-grain wraps

4 ounces fresh herb or garlic goat cheese, crumbled

Lemon wedges, for serving

1. In a large bowl, toss together mushrooms, red pepper, and green beans with 1 tablespoon olive oil and salt.

2. Preheat air fryer to 390°F to 400°F. Air-fry vegetables in 2 batches, 8 to 10 minutes per batch, stirring a few times.

3. Meanwhile, mash chickpeas with lemon juice, remaining 1 tablespoon oil, and pepper; spread on wraps.

4. Divide veggies among wraps; top each with 1 ounce crumbled goat cheese. Fold to wrap. Serve with lemon wedges.

SERVES 4: About 460 calories, 19g protein, 62g carbohydrates, 17g fat (5g saturated), 14g fiber, 836mg sodium.

Buttermilk Fried Chicken

Here's the *real* reason you invested in the air fryer—
guilt-free "fried" chicken, any time you want!

PREP: 25 MINUTES   TOTAL: 1 HOUR, PLUS CHILLING

**10 small pieces chicken (3 pounds),
breasts cut into halves**

1½ cups buttermilk

3 tablespoons cayenne pepper hot sauce

1 teaspoon garlic powder

2 teaspoons salt

1 teaspoon pepper

2 cups all-purpose flour

2 large eggs

Oil in mister

**Hot Honey Sauce (recipe below), for serving
(optional)**

Hot Honey Sauce

Microwave ¼ **cup honey** on 50 percent
power 30 seconds, or just until runny. Whisk
in **2 tablespoons cayenne pepper hot sauce**.
Makes about ⅓ cup.

TIP

Using eggs helps the coating stick and not
flake off. It's best to coat the chicken right
before cooking, instead of coating it all at
once, so it doesn't get too soggy. Make sure
the chicken pieces have space between them
in the air fryer and are placed in a single
layer so pieces don't stick together.

1. Place a 1-gallon resealable plastic bag in a
large bowl. Place chicken in the bag.

2. In another bowl, whisk buttermilk, hot
sauce, garlic powder, and 1 teaspoon salt.
Pour over chicken in bag; seal bag. Refrigerate
3 to 5 hours.

3. Place flour and 1 teaspoon each salt and
pepper in another 1-gallon resealable bag.
Shake to mix. In a shallow bowl, beat eggs
with 2 tablespoons water. Drain chicken.

4. Preheat air fryer to 370°F to 375°F. Spray
air fryer basket with oil. Place chicken, one
piece at a time, in the bag with flour; shake to
coat. Shake off excess flour and dredge in egg,
letting excess drip off. Return to flour, dredge,
and shake off excess. Spray chicken all over with
oil. Working in batches, air-fry 3 to 4 pieces of
chicken at a time, for 20 minutes, or until chicken
is cooked (165°F), turning once. Transfer chicken
to a wire rack set over a baking sheet. Keep
warm in a 250°F oven, if desired. Repeat coating
and air-frying the remaining chicken pieces.

5. Drizzle with Hot Sauce Honey, if desired.

SERVES 5: About 505 calories, 43g protein,
34g carbohydrates, 21g fat (6g saturated), 1g fiber,
638mg sodium.

Ultimate Fried Chicken Sandwich

Secure sandwiches with picks. The close proximity and force of the fan can move bread and other lightweight items. Place toothpicks at an angle to ensure that they stay put. See photo on page 44.

PREP: 15 MINUTES TOTAL: 35 MINUTES

4 small skinless, boneless chicken thighs (about 1½ pounds)

¾ cup low-fat buttermilk

2 teaspoons garlic powder

¾ teaspoon salt

½ teaspoon pepper

¾ cup panko bread crumbs

1 tablespoon vegetable oil or canola oil

1 cup all-purpose flour

4 potato rolls

Shredded romaine, sliced tomatoes, sliced pickles, and hot sauce

1. In a large bowl, combine chicken, buttermilk, garlic powder, and ½ teaspoon each salt and pepper. Marinate in the refrigerator for 1 hour. Crush bread crumbs in a bag with a rolling pin. Place bread crumbs in a shallow dish and toss with oil until evenly coated. Place flour in another shallow dish. One at a time, remove chicken thighs from the buttermilk, allowing excess to drip off. Dip each one in flour, then in buttermilk, then in bread crumbs. Place on a board.

2. Preheat air fryer to 325°F. Place chicken in the basket and air-fry for 15 to 20 minutes or until golden brown and chicken is cooked through (165°F). Sprinkle with ¼ teaspoon salt.

3. Serve on rolls, topped with romaine, tomato, pickles, and hot sauce or other topping combos.

SERVES 4: About 575 calories, 39g protein, 67g carbohydrates, 15g fat (3g saturated), 2g fiber, 622mg sodium.

CHICKEN SANDWICH TOPPING COMBOS

¼ cup honey + ½ teaspoon cayenne + sliced pickles

½ cup chipotle mayo + sliced tomato + shredded cabbage (pictured)

½ cup ranch dressing + 2–3 tablespoons hot sauce + ¼ cup crumbled blue cheese + sliced red onion

---

¼ cup pesto + 4 slices provolone + ¼ cup chopped pepperoncini

---

¼ cup relish of choice + ¼ cup chopped sweet onion + butter lettuce

Spanish Chicken & Peppers

Feeding a family of four? You can easily double this recipe, but you'll have to air-fry everything in two batches.

PREP: **10 MINUTES**   TOTAL: **35 MINUTES**

1¼ pounds assorted small chicken parts, (breasts cut into halves)

½ pound mini sweet peppers

2 teaspoons olive oil

¼ teaspoon salt

¼ teaspoon pepper

¼ cup light mayonnaise

½ clove garlic, crushed with press

¼ teaspoon smoked paprika

Baguette, for serving

1. Preheat air fryer to 375°F. In a large bowl, toss chicken and peppers with oil, salt, and pepper.

2. Arrange peppers in the air fryer basket and top with chicken. Air-fry for 10 minutes. Remove peppers to plate. Turn chicken and air-fry for 10 to 12 minutes longer, or until chicken is cooked (165°F). Remove chicken and return peppers to air fryer. Air-fry for 2 minutes, or until hot.

3. Stir together mayonnaise, garlic, and paprika. Serve chicken and peppers with garlic mayo on a baguette.

SERVES 2: About 500 calories, 38g protein, 10g carbohydrates, 33g fat (7g saturated), 3g fiber, 545mg sodium.

Chicken Caprese

For a healthier take on fried chicken, serve it with fresh tomatoes, mozzarella, basil, and broccolini.

PREP: 10 MINUTES   **TOTAL:** 25 MINUTES

3 teaspoons olive oil

¼ teaspoon salt

1 cup grape tomatoes, halved

⅛ teaspoon pepper, plus a pinch

1 clove garlic, crushed with press

2 chicken breast cutlets (about 10 ounces)

4 ounces fresh mozzarella balls, halved

Fresh basil

1 bunch broccolini, steamed, for serving

1. Preheat air fryer to 390°F to 400°F. In a bowl, toss tomatoes with garlic, 1 teaspoon oil, and a pinch of salt and pepper. Place in basket and air-fry for 3 to 4 minutes, or until tomatoes soften and some burst. Remove from basket and set aside.

2. Brush chicken with the remaining 1 teaspoon oil, and sprinkle with ⅛ teaspoon each salt and pepper. Air-fry for 5 to 6 minutes, or until cooked through. Transfer cutlets to a plate and top with tomatoes, mozzarella, and fresh basil.

3. Serve chicken with steamed broccolini.

SERVES 2: About 430 calories, 43g protein, 11g carbohydrates, 24g fat (10g saturated), 4g fiber, 381mg sodium.

Prosciutto-Wrapped Chicken with Roasted Squash

When it comes to "roasting" vegetables, this is where the air fryer really shines.

PREP: 10 MINUTES   TOTAL: 50 MINUTES

1 small acorn squash, peeled, seeded, and sliced

2 teaspoons olive oil

1 teaspoon fresh thyme leaves, chopped

¼ teaspoon salt

2 boneless, skinless chicken breasts (about 1 pound)

¼ teaspoon pepper

1 tablespoon grated Parmesan cheese

4 slices prosciutto

Sautéed green beans, for serving

1. Preheat air fryer to 375°F. Toss together acorn squash with olive oil, thyme, and salt. Place in air fryer basket. Air-fry for 15 minutes, or until tender, shaking basket once. Put squash in a bowl.

2. Meanwhile, season chicken breasts with pepper; sprinkle with Parmesan. Wrap each with 2 slices prosciutto. Bake 20 minutes in the air fryer, or until cooked through (165°F).

3. Place squash on top of chicken and air-fry for 3 minutes, or until heated.

4. Serve chicken and squash with sautéed green beans.

SERVES 2: About 425 calories, 56g protein, 19g carbohydrates, 14g fat (4g saturated), 6g fiber, 1,059mg sodium.

TIP

Substitute boneless skinless chicken thighs for the breasts if you prefer dark meat.

Mahogany Chicken & Broccoli

Chicken thighs are juicier, cheaper, and easier to cook than breasts.

3 tablespoons low-sodium soy sauce

1 tablespoon balsamic vinegar

2 teaspoons peeled and grated fresh ginger

2 cloves garlic, crushed with press

2 tablespoons honey

4 bone-in chicken thighs (about 2 pounds), fat and excess skin trimmed

1 pound broccoli florets, cut in half if large

1 bunch green onions, cut into 2-inch lengths

1 tablespoon vegetable oil

1. Combine soy sauce, balsamic vinegar, ginger, garlic, and 1 tablespoon honey in a small dish. Place all but 1 tablespoon of the soy mixture in a food storage bag. Add chicken skin side up, push out air, and seal. Refrigerate for 1 hour. Stir the remaining 1 tablespoon of honey into the 1 tablespoon of marinade on the dish as a glaze. Set aside.

2. Preheat air fryer to 375°F. Place chicken in basket, skin side down. Air-fry chicken for 12 minutes. Brush chicken with soy-honey glaze and flip over, using tongs. Air-fry for 10 more minutes until chicken is cooked through (165°F), brushing twice with glaze during the last 3 minutes of cooking. Place on plate and tent with foil.

3. Meanwhile, place broccoli in a microwavable bowl, cover with plastic wrap, and microwave 3 minutes on High. Toss in green onions and oil. Place in air fryer basket and air-fry for 7 minutes, or until tender and lightly roasted, shaking basket once.

4. Serve broccoli with chicken.

SERVES 4: About 420 calories, 35g protein, 19g carbohydrates, 23g fat (6g saturated), 4g fiber, 601mg sodium.

Turkey Burgers with Sweet Potato Fries

Made with ground turkey, and barely any oil, these burgers are a better-for-you alternative to those you'll find at a fast-food joint.

PREP: 15 MINUTES   TOTAL: 40 MINUTES

1 pound ground turkey breast

2 cloves garlic, pressed

½ cup chopped cilantro

1 teaspoon chili powder

¼ teaspoon salt

Oil in mister

½ avocado

2 teaspoons lime juice

4 toasted whole-grain sandwich thins

Tomato, cucumber, lettuce, and sprouts, for serving (optional)

Sweet Potato Fries, for serving (page 107)

1. Mix turkey with garlic, cilantro, chili powder, and salt. Form into 4 (3½-inch) patties. Make a slight indentation in the center of each one. Spray patties on both sides with oil.

2. Preheat air fryer to 370°F. Air-fry in batches (2 at a time), 10 to 12 minutes, or until cooked through (165°F), turning once.

3. Mash avocado with lime juice.

4. Place burgers on whole-grain sandwich thins; top with avocado and tomato, cucumber, lettuce, and sprouts, as desired. Serve with Sweet Potato Fries.

SERVES 4: About 265 calories, 33g protein, 25g carbohydrates, 6g fat (1g saturated), 7g fiber, 395mg sodium.

TIP

Any ground turkey works in this recipe, but ground turkey breast with some dark meat mixed in makes for juicier burgers.

Mozzarella-Stuffed Turkey Meatballs

Psst! We snuck gooey, melty cheese into these meatballs to make them even *more* decadent.

PREP: 25 MINUTES TOTAL: 45 MINUTES

20 ounces ground turkey

⅓ cup Italian seasoned bread crumbs

3 tablespoons milk

1 large egg

3 cloves garlic, finely chopped

1 tablespoon loosely packed fresh rosemary leaves, finely chopped

¼ teaspoon salt

⅛ teaspoon pepper

4 ounces part-skim mozzarella, cut into ½-inch cubes

Oil in mister

2 cups marinara sauce

Parsley leaves and grated Parmesan cheese, for garnish

Bread or cooked pasta, for serving

1. In a large bowl, combine turkey, bread crumbs, milk, egg, garlic, rosemary, salt, and pepper. With a 2-tablespoon scoop, scoop turkey mixture and press 1 cube mozzarella into center, sealing meat tightly around cheese. Repeat with the remaining turkey mixture and cheese.

2. Preheat air fryer to 375°F. Spray basket with oil. Working in batches, add half the turkey meatballs to basket, spacing them ½ inch apart. Air-fry for 8 minutes, or until golden. Meanwhile, heat marinara sauce in a medium-size saucepan. Add meatballs and simmer 12 minutes, or until meatballs are cooked through (165°F).

3. Garnish with parsley and Parmesan. Serve with bread or over pasta.

SERVES 6: About 305 calories, 28g protein, 17g carbohydrates, 14g fat (5g saturated), 2g fiber, 975mg sodium.

Greek-Style Meatballs

It is important to choose leaner ground beef for this recipe. When we tried these meatballs with a higher fat percentage, they turned out too brown and crusty.

PREP: 20 MINUTES   TOTAL: 50 MINUTES

1 pound red potatoes, cut into 1-inch chunks

2 teaspoons olive oil

½ teaspoon salt

⅜ teaspoon pepper

1 pound lean ground beef (90%)

¾ cup crumbled feta cheese

½ small red onion, grated

⅓ cup Italian seasoned bread crumbs

¼ cup chopped fresh parsley leaves

1 large egg, lightly beaten

2 teaspoons dried oregano

½ cup prepared tzatziki sauce

Lemon slices and parsley, for serving

1. Preheat air fryer to 400°F. In a medium-size bowl, toss potatoes with oil, ¼ teaspoon salt, and ⅛ teaspoon pepper. Air-fry 14 minutes, or until browned and cooked through, tossing a few times. Remove potatoes to a plate.

2. In a large bowl, mix ground beef, feta, red onion, bread crumbs, parsley, egg, oregano and ¼ teaspoon each salt and pepper. Form into 12 balls (about ¼ cup each) and thread onto skewers.

3. Reduce air fryer temperature to 375°F. Air-fry meatballs for 10 minutes, or until cooked through. Remove to a plate. Return potatoes to air fryer. Air-fry for 2 minutes, or until hot.

4. Serve with tzatziki and lemon slices. Garnish with additional parsley.

SERVES 4: About 480 calories, 34g protein, 35g carbohydrates, 23g fat (10g saturated), 3g fiber, 1,165mg sodium.

TIP

Six-inch wooden skewers can fit in the air fryer. Soak them for 15 minutes in cold water. However, the meatballs may also be cooked in the air fryer basket without being skewered.

Mustard-Crusted Mini Meat Loaves with Roasted Apples

We snuck in a healthy helping of zucchini for
extra flavor, moisture, and heartiness.

PREP: 15 MINUTES   TOTAL: 40 MINUTES

**3 small Gala or Empire apples, cored
and cut into 8 wedges**

1 teaspoon fresh rosemary, chopped

¼ teaspoon cayenne (ground red) pepper

2 teaspoons olive oil

½ teaspoon salt, plus a pinch

**1 pound ground meat (beef or dark-meat
turkey)**

1 small zucchini, grated (about 5 ounces)

⅓ cup seasoned bread crumbs

¼ teaspoon pepper

2 tablespoons Dijon mustard

Snipped chives, for serving

1. Preheat air fryer to 370°F to 375°F. Toss apples with rosemary, cayenne pepper, olive oil, and a pinch of salt. Air-fry for 10 minutes, or until just tender and lightly browned, tossing a few times. Remove apples and place them on a plate.

2. In a large bowl, combine ground meat, zucchini, bread crumbs, ½ teaspoon salt, pepper, and ¼ cup water. Form into 4 oval-shaped loaves (3½ x 2-inch). Pour ½ cup water into air fryer. Place loaves in basket. Air-fry for 15 minutes. Spread with mustard and air-fry for 5 to 10 minutes more, or until cooked (165°F). Remove meat loaves and place them on a plate. Return apples to the basket and air-fry for 4 minutes, or until hot.

3. Garnish meat loaves with chives and serve with the apples.

SERVES 4: About 310 calories, 25g protein, 24g carbohydrates, 13g fat (6g saturated), 4g fiber, 650mg sodium.

TIP

Use a spoon to spread the mustard onto each meat loaf. It works better than brushing.

Fast Steak Frites

Achieve steakhouse-quality results *without* the
outdoor grill or butter-laden skillet.

PREP: 15 MINUTES   TOTAL: 35 MINUTES

½ **pound russet or Yukon gold potatoes**

1½ **teaspoons vegetable oil**

½ **teaspoon salt**

⅝ **teaspoon pepper**

2 **tablespoons mayonnaise**

¼ **small shallot, finely chopped**

1 **teaspoon lemon juice**

½ **teaspoon finely chopped fresh tarragon,
    plus more for garnish**

2 **thin (⅜-inch-thick) boneless top sirloin
    steaks (about 12 ounces)**

1. Cut potatoes into ¼-inch sticks; soak in water
for 10 minutes. Drain and pat dry. Toss potatoes,
oil, and ¼ teaspoon each salt and pepper.

2. Preheat air fryer to 375°F. Place potatoes in
basket and air-fry for 15 minutes, shaking basket
twice during cooking.

3. Meanwhile, combine mayonnaise, shallot,
1 teaspoon water, lemon juice, tarragon, and
⅛ teaspoon pepper.

4. Preheat air fryer to 400°F. Season steaks
with ¼ teaspoon each salt and pepper. Air-fry
for 6 minutes for medium rare, turning halfway
during cooking. Place steaks on a board to rest
for 2 minutes. Place potatoes in the basket and
air-fry for 2 minutes to warm.

5. Serve fries with steak and mayo. Garnish with
chopped tarragon.

SERVES 2: About 490 calories, 38g protein,
22g carbohydrates, 27g fat (7g saturated), 2g fiber,
650mg sodium.

Hoisin Barbecue Country Pork Ribs

Cook up finger-lickin' ribs—in a fraction of the time!

PREP: 15 MINUTES   TOTAL: 45 MINUTES, PLUS MARINATING

⅓ cup soy sauce

⅓ cup apple cider vinegar

2 tablespoons brown sugar

1 teaspoon ground ginger

½ teaspoon garlic powder

4 bone-in country-style pork ribs (about 2 pounds)

3 tablespoons barbecue sauce

2 tablespoons Hoisin sauce

Slaw, for serving

Sesame seeds, for garnish (optional)

1. Combine soy sauce, vinegar, sugar, ginger, garlic powder, and ¼ cup water in a heavy food storage bag. Add ribs, shake to combine, push out all air, and seal. Marinate in the refrigerator for 2 to 8 hours; turn over bag occasionally. Drain well and discard marinade. In a small bowl, stir together barbecue sauce and Hoisin.

2. Preheat air fryer to 350°F. Place ribs in basket, overlapping if needed. Air-fry for 30 minutes, turning over ribs using tongs every 10 minutes and brushing lightly with the Hoisin-BBQ sauce. Brush with the remaining sauce.

3. Serve with slaw. Garnish with sesame seeds, if desired.

SERVES 4: About 510 calories, 28g protein, 11g carbohydrates, 38g fat (14g saturated), 0g fiber, 547mg sodium.

TIP

Because the temperature in air fryers remains fairly constant, feel free to open the basket and check on your food for doneness.

Bacon-Wrapped Pork Tenderloin

Cook up this beautiful roast for a dinner party. Bonus!
You'll have more space in the oven to bake sides.

PREP: 15 MINUTES   TOTAL: 45 MINUTES

7 slices thick-cut bacon

2 tablespoons packed fresh parsley

1 large scallion

½ teaspoon dried tarragon

2 tablespoons Dijon mustard

⅛ teaspoon pepper

1 boneless pork tenderloin (about 1¼ pounds), silver skin removed

1. Arrange bacon slices in a row on a sheet of plastic wrap (overlap slightly to make a rectangle the length of the tenderloin). Chop together parsley, scallions, and tarragon. Combine mustard, chopped herb mixture, and pepper. Place pork across lower third of bacon; brush pork with mustard mixture. Using the plastic as a guide, roll bacon around the pork. Cut pork in half crosswise.

2. Preheat air fryer to 350°F. Place pork in basket and air-fry for 30 minutes until cooked through (145°F).

3. Let rest 10 minutes and slice.

SERVES 4: About 220 calories, 34g protein, 1g carbohydrates, 8g fat (3g saturated), 0g fiber, 463mg sodium.

Sausage Calzones

This fast and easy meal makes the most of store-bought sausages, sauce, and pizza dough.

PREP: 15 MINUTES   TOTAL: 30 MINUTES

1 cup part-skim ricotta cheese

1 link (3 ounces) fully cooked Italian chicken sausage, diced

¾ cup frozen peas

½ cup shredded part-skim mozzarella cheese

1 package (1 pound) refrigerated pizza dough

1 cup marinara sauce, warmed

1. In a medium-size bowl, stir together ricotta, sausage, frozen peas, and mozzarella.

2. Divide dough into 4 pieces. Using fingertips, press each piece of dough into a 7-inch-wide oval.

3. Place ¼ of the ricotta filling on half of each piece of dough. Brush rim of dough with water and fold other half of dough over filling. Pinch edges together to seal. Repeat with remaining filling and dough.

4. Preheat air fryer to 360°F. Working in batches, place 2 calzones in basket. Air-fry for 12 minutes, or until browned and heated through, turning over halfway during cooking with tongs.

5. Serve with marinara sauce.

SERVES 4: About 470 calories, 22g protein, 60g carbohydrates, 14g fat (5g saturated), 4g fiber, 1,440mg sodium.

TIP

When cooking fatty foods, such as sausages, burgers, and bacon, add about ½ cup water to the pan, to prevent smoking.

Hot Dogs with Toppers

Enjoy the crispiness of classic summer dogs *without* turning on the grill.

PREP: 10 MINUTES   TOTAL: 15 MINUTES

4 bun-length hot dogs

4 hot dog buns

Toppings (see right)

Preheat air fryer to 390°F. Place hot dogs in air fryer basket. Air-fry for 6 minutes or until lightly browned and heated. Serve on a bun with a topping of your choice.

SERVES 4: About 285 calories, 10g protein, 23g carbohydrates, 17g fat (6g saturated), 1g fiber, 637mg sodium.

HOT DOG TOPPERS

Classic Dog

2 tablespoons sweet stewed onions + 1 tablespoon sauerkraut + 1 tablespoon yellow mustard

_____

Italian Dog

1 ounce sautéed peppers and onions + 1 ounce roasted potato chunks

_____

Sonoran Dog

2 tablespoons fresh pico de gallo + 1 tablespoon pickled or fresh jalapeños + 1 tablepsoon sour cream + cilantro

_____

Cuban Frita Dog

2 tablespoons potato sticks + 1½ tablespoons raw chopped white onion + 1 tablespoon ketchup

_____

Hawaiian Dog

2 teaspoons yellow mustard + 1 tablespoon garlic mayo + 2 tablespoons finely chopped fresh pineapple + 1 tablespoon sliced green onions

CLASSIC
DOG

ITALIAN
DOG

SONORAN
DOG

CUBAN FRITA
DOG

HAWAIIAN
DOG

ROASTED SWEET & SOUR
BRUSSELS SPROUTS
(PAGE 101)

3 | Side Dishes

Save some oven space on Thanksgiving, or any day of the year. Almost anything you would roast in a conventional oven can also be cooked in the air fryer. Root vegetables, like potatoes, carrots, radishes, and turnips, still get caramelized and crispy. Brussels sprouts, acorn squash, and cauliflower transform into standout sides when tossed with tangy vinegars, fresh herbs, and spices. Forgo croutons and use the air fryer to crisp up slices of beets or fried green tomatoes for salads. And, of course, French fries (whether store-bought or homemade) cook up perfectly in the air fryer —with little to no oil.

Spicy Acorn Squash with Feta

A couple pantry-staple spices and some feta cheese make this simple side centerpiece-worthy. See photo on page 8.

PREP: 15 MINUTES   **TOTAL: 35 MINUTES**

2 small acorn squash (about 2 pounds), halved, seeded, and sliced (¾ inch thick)

1½ tablespoons olive oil

½ teaspoon smoked paprika

⅛ teaspoon ground red (cayenne) pepper

¼ teaspoon salt

3 fresh sage leaves, finely chopped

¼ cup crumbled feta cheese (about 1 ounce)

1. Preheat air fryer to 380°F. In a large bowl, toss squash, oil, paprika, red pepper, and salt.

2. Place squash in the air fryer basket. Air-fry for 20 minutes, turning slices with tongs a few times, or until tender and lightly browned.

3. Transfer squash to a serving platter; sprinkle with sage and feta.

SERVES 4: About 160 calories, 3g protein, 23g carbohydrates, 7g fat (2g saturated), 7g fiber, 212mg sodium.

TIP

Place a heatproof trivet or cutting board next to your air fryer. When taking out the basket and pan, you will want a safe spot to set down the basket assembly.

Herb-Roasted Root Vegetables

Rich in color and flavor, these root veggies, dressed in thyme and parsley, make for the perfect side dish. See photo on page 6.

PREP: 15 MINUTES   TOTAL: 50 MINUTES

1 pound mixed baby potatoes, cut into halves

½ pound thin baby carrots (halved, if large)

4 large radishes, trimmed, cut into halves

2 tablespoons olive oil

½ teaspoon salt

¼ teaspoon pepper

1 tablespoon chopped fresh thyme

2 tablespoons chopped fresh parsley

1. Preheat air fryer to 350°F.

2. In a large bowl, toss potatoes, carrots, and radishes with 1 tablespoon oil, salt, and pepper. Place coated vegetables in basket and air-fry for 20 minutes. Place air-fried vegetables back in the bowl and toss with the remaining tablespoon of oil and the thyme. Return to the basket and air-fry until golden brown and tender, 15 minutes more, shaking basket.

3. Sprinkle with parsley and serve.

SERVES 4 (1 cup each): About 170 calories, 3g protein, 25g carbohydrates, 7g fat (1g saturated), 4g fiber, 305mg sodium.

Crispy Roasted Potatoes with Caper Vinaigrette

A dash of sherry vinegar and a tablespoon or two of capers add some serious flavor to these "roasted" spuds.

PREP: 15 MINUTES   TOTAL: 35 MINUTES

1¼ pounds Yukon gold potatoes, unpeeled, cut into 1-inch chunks

¾ pound sweet potatoes, unpeeled, cut into 1-inch chunks

1 tablespoon salt, plus ¼ teaspoon

3 tablespoons olive oil

2 tablespoons fresh flat-leaf parsley leaves, finely chopped

2 tablespoons sherry vinegar

1½ tablespoons capers, drained and chopped

1½ teaspoons anchovy paste

½ clove garlic, crushed with press

1. In a 4- to 5-quart saucepot, cover Yukon gold and sweet potatoes with cold water. Stir in 1 tablespoon salt. Partially cover and heat to boiling on high. Reduce heat to maintain simmer; cook 6 minutes, stirring occasionally. Drain well; return to pot. Potatoes can be parboiled and kept at room temperature up to 2 hours before roasting.

2. Preheat air fryer to 390°F. Vigorously toss potatoes with 2 tablespoons oil.

3. Place potatoes in air fryer basket. Air-fry for 20 minutes, shaking basket occasionally, until potatoes are browned and crisp.

4. Meanwhile, in a large bowl, whisk parsley, vinegar, capers, anchovy paste, garlic, remaining 1 tablespoon oil, and ¼ teaspoon salt. Toss potatoes with vinaigrette until well coated.

5. Serve at once while crispy and hot.

SERVES 4: About 290 calories, 5g protein, 43g carbohydrates, 11g fat (1g saturated), 4g fiber, 447mg sodium.

Roasted Beet & Pistachio Salad

Forgo the croutons and top greens with a healthier alternative—crunchy nuts and crispy beets—instead.

PREP: 15 MINUTES   TOTAL: 40 MINUTES

2 medium-size beets (about 6 ounces each)

2 tablespoons shelled, unsalted pistachios

1 tablespoon balsamic vinegar

½ teaspoon Dijon mustard

⅛ teaspoon salt

⅛ teaspoon pepper

2 tablespoons extra-virgin olive oil

8 cups lightly packed baby greens and herbs mix (about 4 ounces)

3 tablespoons crumbled blue cheese

2 tablespoons packed fresh mint leaves

1. Peel beets and cut into ½-inch chunks. Pile beets on a doubled sheet of foil and wrap to enclose tightly.

2. Preheat air fryer to 390°F. Place foil-wrapped beets in basket and air-fry for 25 to 30 minutes, or until tender. Carefully open foil and let beets cool. Place pistachios in the basket and air-fry for 1 minute, or until toasted; let cool.

3. Prepare dressing: In a small bowl, with a fork or a wire whisk, mix vinegar, mustard, salt, and pepper until blended. In a thin, steady stream, whisk in olive oil until blended.

4. In a medium-size bowl, combine beets and 2 teaspoons dressing. In a large serving bowl, toss greens with remaining dressing until coated. Top with blue cheese, pistachios, and beets. Tear mint leaves over salad.

SERVES 4: About 145 calories, 4g protein, 9g carbohydrates, 11g fat (2g saturated), 3g fiber, 223mg sodium.

Roasted Sweet & Sour Brussels Sprouts

When air-fried and paired with a balsamic-soy sauce, this "least beloved" vegetable transforms into a standout side dish. See photo on page 94.

PREP: 10 MINUTES   TOTAL: 35 MINUTES

1 pound Brussels sprouts, trimmed and halved

1 tablespoon olive oil

2 tablespoons low-sodium soy sauce

2 tablespoons balsamic vinegar

1 tablespoon brown sugar

¼ teaspoon ground ginger

⅛ teaspoon pepper

2 tablespoons loosely packed fresh parsley leaves, finely chopped

1. Toss together Brussels sprouts, oil, and 3 tablespoons water.

2. Preheat air fryer to 350°F. Line air fryer basket with a piece of foil cut to fit. Add Brussels sprouts to basket. Air-fry for 15 to 20 minutes, tossing a few times, until tender and browned.

3. Meanwhile, in a 2-cup glass measuring cup, combine soy sauce, vinegar, brown sugar, ginger, and pepper. Microwave on High, 2 to 2½ minutes, or until syrupy.

4. Toss sprouts with parsley and enough sauce to coat. Serve remaining sauce on the side.

SERVES 4: About 100 calories, 4g protein, 15g carbohydrates, 4g fat (1g saturated), 4g fiber, 317mg sodium.

TIP

Don't forget the water! Without H_2O, the sprouts come out tough, dry, and leathery.

Chimichurri Cauliflower "Steaks"

With this trendy veggie getting riced, mashed, and turned into pizza crust, it's important to not forget how delicious it tastes when simply roasted.

PREP: 10 MINUTES   TOTAL: 20 MINUTES

1 large head cauliflower (about 2 pounds)

1 teaspoon ground cumin

3 tablespoons canola oil

⅜ teaspoon salt

¼ cup loosely packed cilantro, finely chopped

¼ cup loosely packed parsley, finely chopped

3 tablespoons red wine vinegar

1 small clove garlic, crushed with press

1 jalapeño, seeded and finely chopped

1. Quarter the cauliflower and slice into ¾-inch slabs. Combine cumin, 1 tablespoon oil, and ¼ teaspoon salt in a large bowl. Toss in cauliflower until evenly coated.

2. Preheat air fryer to 390°F. Place cauliflower in basket and air-fry until tender and browned, 16 minutes, shaking basket twice during cooking.

3. Meanwhile, stir together cilantro, parsley, vinegar, garlic, jalapeño, remaining 2 tablespoons oil, and ⅛ teaspoon salt.

4. Serve cauliflower with herb sauce.

SERVES 4 (1 cup each): About 120 calories, 2g protein, 5g carbohydrates, 11g fat (1g saturated), 2g fiber, 211mg sodium.

Fried Green Tomatoes

Enjoy this Southern favorite (sans the guilt!) over salad
greens or stacked in between two slices of bread.

PREP: 15 MINUTES   TOTAL: 35 MINUTES

2 tablespoons apple cider vinegar

1½ tablespoons olive oil

⅞ teaspoon salt, plus more for seasoning

⅛ teaspoon pepper

3 tablespoons finely chopped roasted
red peppers

1½ tablespoons capers, chopped

⅓ cup all-purpose flour

1 large egg, beaten

1 cup panko bread crumbs

2 medium green tomatoes (12 ounces),
cored, ends trimmed and discarded,
cut into ¼-inch-thick slices

Oil in mister

3 cups loosely packed baby kale
and microgreens

3 tablespoons crumbled blue cheese

1. Prepare vinaigrette: Whisk vinegar, olive oil,
and ⅛ teaspoon each salt and black pepper;
stir in red peppers and capers. Set aside.

2. Prepare tomatoes: Place flour in 1 large
shallow bowl; place eggs in another. Place panko
and ½ teaspoon salt in a third bowl. Sprinkle
tomato slices with ¼ teaspoon salt. Dredge
tomato slices in flour, then egg, letting excess
drip off. Dredge in panko, patting so crumbs
adhere. Place on a board and spray with oil.

3. Preheat air fryer to 390°F. Working in
batches, place half the tomatoes in basket, oil
side down. Spray with oil. Air-fry until golden
brown, 10 minutes. Using tongs, transfer
tomatoes to a board and season lightly with salt.

4. Warm the tomatoes by inverting the previous
batch onto the tomatoes in basket, and air-fry
for 2 minutes.

5. Toss greens with 1½ tablespoons vinaigrette.
Place tomatoes on a serving platter; top
with cheese.

6. Serve tomatoes immediately with greens
and remaining vinaigrette.

SERVES 4: About 230 calories, 8g protein,
29g carbohydrates, 9g fat (2g saturated), 3g fiber,
676mg sodium.

Spice-Roasted Carrots

Say goodbye to sad, steamed veggies once and for all. For a pop of color, look for rainbow carrots, sometimes called heirloom carrots.

PREP: 15 MINUTES   TOTAL: 30 MINUTES

6 carrots (about 1¼ pounds), peeled, halved crosswise and lengthwise

1 tablespoon olive oil

1 tablespoon packed fresh oregano leaves, chopped

½ teaspoon smoked paprika

¼ teaspoon ground nutmeg

¼ teaspoon salt

⅛ teaspoon pepper

1 tablespoon butter, melted

1 tablespoon red wine vinegar

2 tablespoons roasted, salted, shelled pistachios, chopped

1. Toss together carrots, oil, oregano, paprika, nutmeg, salt, and pepper.

2. Preheat air fryer to 370°F. Place carrots in air fryer basket. Air-fry for 15 minutes, tossing a few times, until lightly browned and tender.

3. Transfer to a serving platter. Drizzle with butter and vinegar, and sprinkle with pistachios.

SERVES 4: About 135 calories, 3g protein, 14g carbohydrates, 8g fat (6g saturated), 4g fiber, 269mg sodium.

TIP

Don't use large carrots for this recipe; they're tough to fit in the air fryer!

Sweet Potato Fries

For fiery fries, toss the spuds with ¾ teaspoon chili powder in step 2. You can also add your own favorite spices for a flavor boost. See photo on page 79.

PREP: 15 MINUTES   TOTAL: 35 MINUTES

1 pound sweet potatoes (1 large)

¾ teaspoon cornstarch

1½ teaspoons olive oil

¼ teaspoon salt

¾ teaspoon chili powder (optional)

1. Cut sweet potatoes into ¼-inch-wide sticks. Soak in water for 10 minutes; drain well and pat dry. In a bowl, toss potatoes in cornstarch until evenly coated.

2. Preheat air fryer to 375°F. Place potatoes in basket and air-fry for 15 minutes, shaking once. Return to bowl and toss with oil, ¼ teaspoon salt, and chili powder, if using, until evenly coated. Reduce temperature to 300°F. Place in basket and air-fry until tender and golden brown, 7 minutes.

SERVES 4 (1 cup each): About 80 calories, 1g protein, 15g carbohydrates, 2g fat (0g saturated), 3g fiber, 162mg sodium.

TIP

Be sure to remove the basket from the pan if you are pouring out ingredients from the basket. If not, any rendered fats or cooking juices accumulated in the pan will pour out with your air-fried foods.

Summer Veggie Roast

Vegetables become caramelized and crispy in the air fryer, so you shouldn't have trouble convincing the whole family to eat every single one. Plus you won't need to turn on the oven during the warmer months.

PREP: 20 MINUTES   TOTAL: 45 MINUTES

1 medium zucchini, halved lengthwise and cut into ½-inch-thick slices

1 medium yellow or summer squash, halved lengthwise and cut into ½-inch-thick slices

1 large orange or red pepper, cut into 1-inch pieces

½ red onion, cut into thin wedges through root end

1 tablespoon olive oil

¼ teaspoon salt

2 ears corn, kernels cut from cobs

½ cup grape tomatoes, halved

¼ cup packed fresh basil leaves, chopped

1 tablespoon butter

1. Toss together zucchini, yellow squash, orange pepper, onion, olive oil, and salt.

2. Preheat air fryer to 380°F. Place vegetables in basket. Air-fry for 15 minutes, tossing once. Stir in corn and tomatoes. Air-fry for 8 to 10 minutes more, tossing once, or until vegetables are tender.

3. Place vegetables in a serving bowl and stir in basil and butter.

SERVES 4 (1 cup each): About 140 calories, 4g protein, 17g carbohydrates, 7g fat (3g saturated), 3g fiber, 156mg sodium.

TIP

Be sure to keep your air fryer away from close proximity to walls or other surfaces. Fryers vent hot air out the back of the appliance.

Corn on the Cob

Savor sweet, juicy corn *without* having to turn on the grill or stove first.

PREP: 5 MINUTES   TOTAL: 20 MINUTES

4 ears corn on the cob, shucked

Preheat air fryer to 375°F. Trim corn, if needed, to fit air fryer and place in basket. Air-fry 12 minutes, or until tender, turning over with tongs halfway through.

SERVES 4: About 90 calories, 3g protein, 19g carbohydrates, 1g fat (0g saturated), 2g fiber, 15mg sodium.

FUN FLAVORS

Skip the butter and spread one of these condi-ments on your corn instead—**harissa, garlic-herb cheese spread, pimiento cheese**, or **pesto**.

TIP

Whether you're cooking 1 ear of corn or 4, the timing for this recipe is the same.

Twice-Baked Herb-Stuffed Potatoes

Want to know a secret? These cheesy, indulgent potatoes aren't "baked" at all.

PREP: 50 MINUTES   TOTAL: 1 HOUR 35 MINUTES, PLUS COOLING

3 large russet potatoes (2¾ pounds), well scrubbed

1 medium shallot

¼ cup packed fresh basil leaves

4 tablespoons Parmesan cheese

2 tablespoons butter

¼ teaspoon dried marjoram

½ teaspoon salt

½ teaspoon freshly ground black pepper

2 tablespoons low-fat sour cream

⅓ cup 2% milk

1. With fork, pierce each potato 3 times; place on a sheet of parchment paper in the microwave. Microwave on High for 15 minutes, or until tender, turning once. Cover with a kitchen towel; let cool.

2. Meanwhile, finely chop shallots and basil. Grate Parmesan.

3. Combine butter and shallots in a small bowl; cover with plastic. Microwave on High for 1½ minutes, until shallots are softened. Place in a large bowl with marjoram, basil, 3 tablespoons Parmesan, salt, and pepper.

4. Cut potatoes crosswise in half. Trim off the rounded ends so that potatoes stand upright. With a spoon, scoop out potato flesh, leaving ¼-inch shell; place flesh in a bowl. Add sour cream and milk; mash well. Spoon mixture into shells. Top with remaining 1 tablespoon Parmesan.

5. Preheat air fryer to 375°F. Place potatoes in basket using tongs, and air-fry until golden brown and heated through, 12 minutes.

SERVES 6: About 230 calories, 6g protein, 40g carbohydrates, 6g fat (3g saturated), 3g fiber, 254mg sodium.

Polenta Fries

We're turning this comfort dish into a crispy, addictive snack
(with a little help from the air fryer!).

1 tube refrigerated polenta (about 18 ounces)

1 tablespoon olive oil

½ teaspoon basil, crushed

¼ teaspoon oregano, crushed

¼ teaspoon garlic powder

Oil in mister

1 cup jarred Arrabbiata sauce, for dipping

1. Unwrap polenta and cut in half crosswise. Cut each half lengthwise into ½-inch sticks. Combine oil, basil, oregano, and garlic powder in a large bowl; add polenta sticks and toss.

2. Preheat air fryer to 400°F. Spray basket with oil. Add polenta sticks and air-fry until beginning to color, 24 minutes. Shake basket 3 times during cooking. (Fries will crisp after standing for a few minutes.) Meanwhile, warm sauce, covered, in microwave on High for 90 seconds, or until heated through. Serve with polenta fries.

SERVES 4: About 150 calories, 4g protein, 24g carbohydrates, 4g fat (0g saturated), 2g fiber, 603mg sodium.

TIP

The basket gets hot! Use silicone-coated oven mitts or tongs to remove or add foods to the preheated basket.

COCONUT FRENCH TOAST
(PAGE 123)

4 | Sweets & Desserts

Bring out the air fryer to "bake" up some of your favorite desserts. We adapted a few of our favorite sweet recipes, so you can make French toast, fruit crumbles, and Chocolate Molten Cakes, without having to worry whether it'll work or not. Thanks to store-bought biscuit dough and puff pastry, you're just three ingredients away from Cocoa Croissants or jelly-filled doughnuts. We even figured out how to whip up apple pies! The secret? Ditching the pie pan, using ramekins, microwaving the apples, and making them mini, so they cook faster.

Shortcut Jelly Doughnuts

Hot, fresh doughnuts? Now that's our jam. Make them at home, in minutes, with our fried-and-true recipe.

PREP: 10 MINUTES   TOTAL: 25 MINUTES

1 package (16.3 ounces) large refrigerator biscuits

Oil in mister

1¼ cups good-quality raspberry jam

Confectioners' sugar for dusting

1. Separate biscuits into 8 rounds. Spray both sides of rounds lightly with oil.

2. Preheat air fryer to 350°F. Spray basket with oil and place 3 to 4 rounds in basket. Air-fry for 5 minutes, or until golden brown. Transfer to a wire rack; let cool. Repeat with the remaining rounds.

3. Fill a pastry bag, fitted with small plain tip, with raspberry jam; use tip to poke a small hole in the side of each doughnut, then fill the centers with the jam. Dust doughnuts with confectioners' sugar.

SERVES 8: About 305 calories, 3g protein, 59g carbohydrates, 6g fat (3g saturated), 1g fiber, 458mg sodium.

TIP

Air fryer temperatures can vary by manufacturer. Use the temperature setting closest to the one suggested in the recipe.

Fresh Fruit Crumble

Keep the cinnamon-sweet crumb topping in the freezer, so you can whip up this dessert whenever you have an abundance of fresh, seasonal fruit.

PREP: 10 MINUTES   TOTAL: 55 MINUTES

1½ pounds baking apples (such as Gala) or firm-ripe pears

2 tablespoons brown sugar

½ teaspoon pie spice

1 teaspoon grated fresh ginger

2 teaspoons fresh lemon juice

½ cup all-purpose flour

CRUMB TOPPING

½ cup old-fashioned oats

¼ cup packed brown sugar

1 teaspoon finely grated lemon peel

¾ teaspoon apple pie spice

⅛ teaspoon salt

5 tablespoons butter, cut up

Vanilla ice cream or whipped cream, for topping

1. Preheat air fryer to 375°F. Fold a 20-inch piece of foil lengthwise into a 2-inch-wide strip to use as a sling. In a bowl, toss fruit with sugar, pie spice, ginger, and lemon juice. Place in a 1-quart round (5-inch diameter) baking/food storage dish. Using the foil sling, place the dish in the air fryer basket. Fold down the foil "handles" over the dish, keeping it away from the element. Air-fry for 25 minutes, stirring twice. Press fruit down with the back of a wooden spoon to compact.

2. Prepare topping: Meanwhile, combine flour, oats, sugar, lemon peel, pie spice, and salt in a bowl. Blend in butter until evenly crumbly.

3. Pull out basket and spoon topping onto hot fruit mixture.

4. Reduce temperature to 300°F. Air-fry for 20 minutes until golden and fruit is tender.

5. Serve with a scoop of vanilla ice cream or whipped cream.

SERVES 5: About 305 calories, 3g protein, 49g carbohydrates, 13g fat (7g saturated), 4g fiber, 146mg sodium.

TIP

Ovenproof glass food storage dishes can be found in most supermarkets, and are made by major bakeware companies. We love Pyrex®.

Individual Apple Pies

Ditch the pie pan! Line ramekins with crust and make mini, personalized pies, because no one *really* likes to share.

PREP: 15 MINUTES   TOTAL: 25 MINUTES, PLUS COOLING

1 refrigerated piecrust (store-bought or see below)

1 pound McIntosh apples

2 tablespoons packed brown sugar

2 tablespoons dried cranberries

2 teaspoons all-purpose flour

½ teaspoon ground cinnamon

⅛ teaspoon grated nutmeg

¼ teaspoon grated orange rind

Pinch salt

Ultimate Pie Dough

In a food processor, pulse **1 cup all-purpose flour** and ¼ **teaspoon salt** until combined. Add **3 tablespoons butter**, cut up and very cold; pulse until fine crumbs form. Add an additional **3 tablespoons butter**, cut up and very cold; pulse until coarse crumbs form. Sprinkle **3 tablespoons ice water** over mixture; pulse until just incorporated. Pulse in additional ice water until dough just holds together when squeezed. Transfer dough to a lightly floured surface; knead gently until dough comes together. Pat into a flat rectangle. Wrap tightly in plastic; refrigerate at least 30 minutes or up to 1 day.

1. Roll piecrust out on a floured surface. Cut out three (4½-inch) rounds with a glass and refrigerate on a baking sheet.

2. Preheat air fryer to 350°F. Peel, core, and cut apples into half-slices. In a microwave-safe bowl, toss apples, brown sugar, cranberries, flour, cinnamon, nutmeg, orange rind, and a pinch of salt. Microwave on High for 2½ minutes or just until softened, stirring once. Divide filling among 3 (6-ounce/3½-inch-diameter) ramekins or custard cups. Place piecrust rounds on top, form a fluted edge, and cut a slit in the center. Place in the air fryer basket and air-fry for 10 to 12 minutes, or until golden brown.

3. Cool 10 minutes and serve warm or at room temperature.

SERVES 3: About 345 calories, 3g protein, 58g carbohydrates, 14g fat (6g saturated), 2g fiber, 336mg sodium.

TIP

Recipe can be doubled. Microwave apples for 6 minutes on High, stirring twice. Bake pies in 2 batches.

Pecan-Stuffed "Baked" Apples

This decadent dessert has all the goodness of apple pie
(even the ice cream—à la mode!), but requires less effort.

PREP: 15 MINUTES   TOTAL: 40 MINUTES

4 Gala or Empire apples (about 1¼ pounds)

¼ cup chopped pecans

⅓ cup dried tart cherries

1 tablespoon melted butter

3 tablespoons brown sugar

¼ teaspoon allspice

Pinch salt

Ice cream, for serving

1. Cut off top ½ inch from each apple; reserve tops. With a melon baller, core through stem ends without breaking through the bottom. (Do not trim bases.)

2. Preheat air fryer to 350°F. Combine pecans, cherries, butter, brown sugar, allspice, and a pinch of salt. Stuff mixture into the hollow centers of the apples. Cover with apple tops. Place in the air fryer basket, using tongs. Air-fry for 20 to 25 minutes, or just until tender.

3. Serve warm, with ice cream.

SERVES 4: About 225 calories, 1g protein, 39g carbohydrates, 8g fat (2g saturated), 4g fiber, 56mg sodium.

TIP

When shopping, look for smaller, narrower apples that will fit in the basket, all in one batch.

Sweet 'n' Salty Maple Granola Bark

Eat these crunchy clusters with milk, yogurt, or ice cream.
Or snack on them by the handful.

PREP: 10 MINUTES   TOTAL: 45 MINUTES

1 large egg white

⅓ cup maple syrup

1 teaspoon vanilla extract

¼ cup olive oil

¼ teaspoon salt

1½ cups old-fashioned oats

½ cup roasted, salted almonds, coarsely chopped

¼ cup sunflower seeds

¼ cup almond flour

¾ teaspoon ground cinnamon

Milk and fresh fruit (such as berries and peaches), for serving (optional)

1. In a small bowl, lightly beat egg white with a fork; measure out 1 tablespoon of the beaten egg white and set aside. Discard the remaining egg white or save for another use.

2. Cut a piece of parchment paper to line the bottom and halfway up the sides of the air fryer, pressing parchment against the sides and the bottom.

3. In a small bowl, combine maple syrup, vanilla, olive oil, salt, and 1 tablespoon beaten egg white. In a large bowl, combine oats, almonds, sunflower seeds, almond flour, and cinnamon. Add the maple syrup mixture to the dry ingredients and mix thoroughly.

4. Evenly press half the mixture (1⅓ cups) into the prepared air fryer basket, using the back of a spoon or wet hands. Place basket in air fryer pan.

5. Air-fry at 325°F for 12 to 16 minutes, or until golden brown all over, not just at the edges. Do not stir.

6. Carefully lift granola out of the air fryer by grabbing the parchment at the sides; let it cool on the parchment on a wire rack for 1 hour before breaking it into chunks. Repeat with the remaining oat mixture.

7. Serve with milk and fruit, if desired. Store in an airtight container at room temperature for up to 1 week.

SERVES 6: About 335 calories, 7g protein, 30g carbohydrates, 22g fat (2g saturated), 4g fiber, 146mg sodium.

TIP

Do not preheat the air fryer for this recipe. You don't want the fryer to be hot when you line it with parchment and press the granola in!

Cocoa Croissants

Here's a reason to always keep a package of puff pastry in the freezer.

PREP: 15 MINUTES   TOTAL: 50 MINUTES

1 sheet frozen puff pastry, thawed

⅓ cup chocolate-hazelnut spread

1 large egg, beaten

1. On lightly floured surface, roll puff pastry into a 14-inch square. Cut pastry into quarters to form 4 squares. Cut each square diagonally to form 8 triangles.

2. Spread 2 teaspoons chocolate-hazelnut spread on each triangle; from wider end, roll up pastry. Brush egg on top of each roll.

3. Preheat air fryer to 375°F. Air-fry rolls in batches, 3 or 4 at a time, 8 minutes per batch, or until pastry is golden brown.

4. Cool on a wire rack; serve while warm or at room temperature.

SERVES 8: About 200 calories, 4g protein, 18g carbohydrates, 12g fat (6g saturated), 1g fiber, 163mg sodium.

Individual Chocolate Molten Cakes

Timing is tricky in the air fryer, but even if cakes are slightly overbaked, they are still delicious—especially when served with ice cream.

PREP: 20 MINUTES   TOTAL: 45 MINUTES, PLUS FOR COOLING

¼ cup butter (½ stick), cut into pieces, plus more for greasing the custard cups

2 tablespoons granulated sugar, plus more for dusting

2 ounces semisweet chocolate, chopped

2 tablespoons heavy or whipping cream

¼ teaspoon vanilla extract

2 tablespoons all-purpose flour

1 large egg

1 large egg yolk

Confectioners' sugar, for dusting

Whipped cream or ice cream, for serving (optional)

1. Grease four 6-ounce custard cups. Dust with granulated sugar.

2. In a heavy 2-quart saucepan, heat chocolate, butter, and cream over low heat, stirring occasionally, until chocolate has melted and mixture is smooth. Remove pan from heat. Add vanilla. Whisk in flour until mixture is smooth.

3. Preheat air fryer to 300°F. In a small bowl, with mixer at high speed, beat 2 tablespoons granulated sugar, whole egg, and egg yolk until thick and pale yellow, about 5 minutes. Fold egg mixture, one-third at a time, into chocolate mixture until blended.

4. Divide batter evenly among prepared custard cups. Air-fry in batches, 2 cups at a time, for 8 to 10 minutes, or until firm at edges and soft in center when pressed lightly.

5. Cool on a wire rack for 5 minutes. Run a thin knife around the sides of the cups to loosen cakes; invert onto plates. Dust with confectioners' sugar.

6. Serve immediately with whipped cream or ice cream, if desired.

SERVES 4: About 290 calories, 4g protein, 22g carbohydrates, 22g fat (13g saturated), 1g fiber, 113mg sodium.

Coconut French Toast

Everyone will go coconuts for this tropical take on a brunch must-have dish. See photo on page 110.

See photo on page 110.

PREP: 15 MINUTES   TOTAL: 45 MINUTES

2 large eggs

¾ cup unsweetened coconut milk

2 tablespoons brown sugar

¼ teaspoon pumpkin pie spice

Pinch salt

4 (1-inch thick) slices brioche or Texas toast

1 cup crispy rice cereal

½ cup unsweetened, finely shredded coconut

Oil in mister

Mixed berries, confectioners' sugar, and maple syrup, for serving (optional)

1. In a shallow 1½-quart baking dish, whisk eggs, coconut milk, brown sugar, pumpkin pie spice, salt. Trim crusts off bread, if desired. Place rice cereal in a shallow bowl and crush with a flat-bottomed dry measuring cup or a glass. Stir in coconut. Dip bread in the egg mixture, coating both sides, for about 10 seconds, then dip into the cereal-coconut mixture, again coating on both sides. Spray tops with oil.

2. Preheat air fryer to 375°F. Working in batches, place bread in air fryer basket, oil side down; spray top with oil. Air-fry for 8 minutes or until golden brown. Transfer to a parchment-lined cookie sheet and keep warm in a 300°F oven.

3. Serve with mixed berries, confectioners' sugar, and maple syrup, if desired.

SERVES 2: About 685 calories, 15g protein, 72g carbohydrates, 40g fat (29g saturated), 6g fiber, 509mg sodium.

TIP

Turn this into French Toast Sticks. Cut bread slices into thirds when trimming crusts in step one and proceed as directed.

Index

Note: Page numbers in *italics* indicate photos separate from recipes.

Photography Credits

Metric Conversion Charts

The recipes that appear in this cookbook use the standard United States method for measuring liquid and dry or solid ingredients (teaspoons, tablespoons, and cups). The information on this chart is provided to help cooks outside the U.S. successfully use these recipes. All equivalents are approximate.

METRIC EQUIVALENTS FOR DIFFERENT TYPES OF INGREDIENTS

STANDARD CUP	FINE POWDER (e.g., flour)	GRAIN (e.g., rice)	GRANULAR (e.g., sugar)	LIQUID SOLIDS (e.g., butter)	LIQUID (e.g., milk)
¾	105 g	113 g	143 g	150 g	180 ml
⅔	93 g	100 g	125 g	133 g	160 ml
½	70 g	75 g	95 g	100 g	120 ml
⅓	47 g	50 g	63 g	67 g	80 ml
¼	35 g	38 g	48 g	50 g	60 ml
⅛	18 g	19 g	24 g	25 g	30 ml

¼ tsp	=					1 ml
½ tsp	=					2 ml
1 tsp	=					5 ml
3 tsp	=	1 tbsp	=	½ fl oz	=	15 ml
		2 tbsp	=	⅛ cup	=	1 fl oz	=	30 ml
		4 tbsp	=	¼ cup	=	2 fl oz	=	60 ml
		5⅓ tbsp	=	⅓ cup	=	3 fl oz	=	80 ml
		8 tbsp	=	½ cup	=	4 fl oz	=	120 ml
		10⅔ tbsp	=	⅔ cup	=	5 fl oz	=	160 ml
		12 tbsp	=	¾ cup	=	6 fl oz	=	180 ml
		16 tbsp	=	1 cup	=	8 fl oz	=	240 ml
		1 pt	=	2 cups	=	16 fl oz	=	480 ml
		1 qt	=	4 cups	=	32 fl oz	=	960 ml
						33 fl oz	=	1000 ml = 1 L

USEFUL EQUIVALENTS FOR DRY INGREDIENTS BY WEIGHT

(To convert ounces to grams, multiply the number of ounces by 30.)

1 oz	=	1/16 lb	=	30 g
2 oz	=	¼ lb	=	120 g
4 oz	=	½ lb	=	240 g
8 oz	=	¾ lb	=	360 g
16 oz	=	1 lb	=	480 g

USEFUL EQUIVALENTS LENGTH

(To convert inches to centimeters, multiply the number of inches by 2.5.)

1 in	=					2.5 cm
6 in	=	½ ft	=			15 cm
12 in	=	1 ft	=			30 cm
36 in	=	3 ft	=	1 yd	=	90 cm
40 in	=					100 cm = 1 m

USEFUL EQUIVALENTS FOR COOKING/OVEN TEMPERATURES

	Fahrenheit	Celsius	Gas Mark
Freeze Water	32°F	0°C	
Room Temperature	68°F	20°C	
Boil Water	212°F	100°C	
Bake	325°F	160°C	3
	350°F	180°C	4
	375°F	190°C	5
	400°F	200°C	6
	425°F	220°C	7
	450°F	230°C	8
Broil			Grill

THE GOOD HOUSEKEEPING
TRIPLE-TEST PROMISE

At *Good Housekeeping,* we want to make sure that every recipe we print works in any oven, with any brand of ingredient, no matter what. That's why, in our test kitchens at the Good Housekeeping Institute, we go all out: We test each recipe at least three times—and, often, several more times after that.

When a recipe is first developed, one member of our team prepares the dish, and we judge it on these criteria: It must be delicious, family-friendly, healthful, and easy to make.

1 The recipe is then tested several more times to fine-tune the flavor and ease of preparation, always by the same team member, using the same equipment.

2 Next, another team member follows the recipe as written, varying the brands of ingredients and kinds of equipment. Even the types of stoves we use are changed.

3 A third team member repeats the whole process using yet another set of equipment and alternative ingredients. By the time the recipes appear on these pages, they are guaranteed to work in any kitchen, including yours. We promise.